#TRADING

MIND MEDICINE FOR TRADERS & INVESTORS

Stephen Hoad

www.thestophunter.co.uk
1st Edition 2016
Copyright © 2016 Stephen Hoad
All rights reserved.
ISBN:- 10: 1540554333
ISBN:- 13: 978-1540554338
Cover Design: Anthony Thornley, Thornley Design.

DISCLAIMER

Please note that Stephen Hoad is not authorised to give financial or tax advice and that commentaries, information and other materials contained in any part of this book are purely educational in nature and are not intended to amount to advice on which reliance should be placed.

They should not be relied upon for the purpose of effecting securities transactions or other investing strategies, nor should they be construed as an offer or solicitation of an offer to sell or buy any security. The author therefore disclaims all liability and responsibility arising from any reliance placed on any information displayed in this book (including without limitation liability and responsibility for any investment decision made), or by anyone who may be informed of any of its contents.

Trading and investing involves a very high degree of risk. Past results are not indicative of future returns and financial instruments can go down as well as up resulting in you receiving less than you invested. Do not assume that any recommendations, insights, charts, theories, or philosophies will ensure profitable investment.

CONTENTS

ABOUT THE AUTHOR 1
FOREWORD 3
INTRODUCTION 5
    The origin of #TradingThought 5
    The world of quotes, proverbs, sayings, idioms and mottos 6
    Why use quotes? 7
    Chinese fortune cookies 8
WHO IS THIS BOOK FOR? 11
HOW THIS BOOK WORKS 13

#TRADINGJOURNEY

LEARNING 20
    Knowledge 20
    Education 21
    Experience 22
YOU 26

#TRADINGDISASTER

FEAR & GREED 32
    Fear 33
    Greed 35
DESTRUCTIVE ACTIONS 36

Ego.. 36

Gossip 37

Gambling.. 37

Mistakes... 38

Luck.. 39

Failure 41

Revenge 43

#TRADINGMINDSET

FUNDAMENTAL APPROACH.. 49

   Committed, hardworking & disciplined 50

   Focused.. 53

   Prepared 56

   Analytical... 57

   Imaginative 57

   Passionate... 58

PERSONALITY TRAITS 60

   Composure.. 61

   Resilience:.. 62

   Positivity.. 64

   Perseverance 66

   Adaptability... 68

   Confidence 69

   Patience... 71

Caution	72
Coolness	72
Consistency	73
Tenacity	74
Rationality	75
Smart thinking & creativity	75
Measured risk taking	78
Psychopathy	80
A MINDSET FOR SUCCESS	83
Dreams	84
Goals	85
Making Money	87
Winners	88
Success	91
Future	92
Hope	94

#TRADINGSKILLS

MARKET THOUGHTS	101
ESSENTIAL SKILLS	105
Risk Management	105
Technical Analysis	106
Statistics and results	108
Strategy and Planning	109

#TRADINGGURUS

LEGENDS 117
    Paul Tudor Jones 117
    George Soros 118
    Warren Buffett 119
    Jesse Livermore 120
BEST OF THE REST 122

#TRADINGWISDOM

JAPANESE 130
CHINESE 132
    Sun Tzu 133
    Lau Tzu 135
    Confucius 135
    Chinese Proverbs 137
GREEK & ROMAN 140

FINAL THOUGHT 143
    Who is the ideal trader or investor? 143
    Are traders and investors two different types of people?
    146
    Are you simply born to trade? 146
    How do you achieve trading and investing glory? 147

Utilising the power of the proverb!................................... 148

GLOSSARY 151
REFERENCES.. 155
BIBLIOGRAPHY 157
ABOUT THE STOP HUNTER 159
THANK YOU 159
READER OFFER..160

INDEX 161

ABOUT THE AUTHOR

Stephen Hoad is a trading and risk management professional and financial markets expert, with more than twenty years' experience on trading floors in the City of London. What makes his career history so unique, is that he has been both the gamekeeper and the poacher; providing him with a rare insight into how the world's financial markets work and are traded.

He started his journey at one of the world's largest American investment banks, in Fixed Income. He then honed his risk and quantitative risk management skills in equities, money markets and commodities at both Japanese and German investment banks, before moving to a role at the world's largest private company – Koch Industries. Here, as a Front Office Risk Manager, he specialised in commodities; designing and optimising global trading and risk strategies.

He then moved over to the trading desk as a fully-fledged options market maker, proprietary trader and technical analyst. He is now a proprietary trader, trading his own funds and strategies, which are based on technical analysis and behavioural science.

Stephen is an economics graduate, who also holds an MSc in Financial Markets & Derivatives and is a fully qualified technical analyst (MSTA) – being one of only a rare few to achieve a distinction level in this vast subject. He specialises in Japanese charting techniques, systematic and automated trading, derivatives products, financial & quantitative theory and risk management. He also has a familiarity with, and understands the nuances of, dealing and trading with China and speaks basic Mandarin.

More recently he founded THE **STOP HUNTER**, a training & consultancy business. He now utilises his considerable expertise in the commodities, forex and equities markets, to educate and train private investors who want to learn to trade the financial markets.

Although retired from the City, he still undertakes consultancy work in technical analysis and systematic trading solutions, for financial institutions and universities. He is regularly a guest speaker at conferences and corporate events and currently leads a Bloomberg outreach programme at Canterbury Christ Church University. He is also on the core panel of lecturers for the Society of Technical Analysts; in the last few years teaching at the London School of Economics and Queen Mary's University, London.

Stephen lives with his wife, Clair and their four children in Kent. A keen triathlete and golfer, he loves watching all sport and reading the odd history book when he gets the spare time!

FOREWORD

Every aspect of life, when approached with the right frame of mind, is easier and usually more enjoyable. This does not just mean a lick of Panglossian positivism, as often a good dose of realism, or even scepticism, goes a long way. The best psychology involves using the correct tools for tackling a specific job; the trick is amassing them in the first place and then choosing appropriately. School and parents will teach you some skills, life itself probably a lot more, but is there a way to take things that bit further?

Stephen Hoad's new book #TradingThought might be just the thing for keen financiers and market punters. He certainly has the years of experience one would expect, with a career spanning both global risk management and trading, and I've known him via the Society of Technical Analysts for many years. His work motivating both professional traders and private investors, through his financial education business THE **STOP HUNTER** led him to this collection of quotes, mottos and idioms.

I too have collected these over many years, as have Bloomberg and others, using them daily. I have always been surprised how very many people love these – usually just for the fun of it – and have helpfully written in with suggestions. Still my favourite is the one from Eleanor Roosevelt who said: 'I think, at a child's birth, if a mother could ask a fairly godmother to endow it with the most useful gift, that gift would be curiosity'.

Nicole Elliott
Freelance financial journalist & private investor.

INTRODUCTION

The origin of #TradingThought

#TradingThought is not a book I ever intended to write. After retiring from the City of London in 2014, I founded my training company THE **STOP HUNTER**, with the aim of bringing the skills and knowledge of the professional trading world to the everyday private investor.

This led me into the world of social media and Twitter. In an effort to educate and inspire my clients and other traders, I found myself posting daily motivational quotes, proverbs, sayings and mottos, with the hashtag TradingThought, alongside real-time market information, news and technical charts.

To my surprise, I noticed that these motivational Tweets were being 're-tweeted' more than any other posts I was putting together. I had assumed that traders and investors, being largely analytical people, would prefer hard facts. However, the Twitter analytics proved otherwise.

From my years working with some of the best traders in the world, as well as training complete novices and observing my own trading, I instinctively knew that psychology plays a huge part in the fine line between success and failure in the financial markets. However, as I dug deeper, I found myself drawn into the world of mindfulness and discovered academic research that also supports the idea that positive emotions can help you think and act smarter – even under stress.

It slowly dawned on me, that although you could spend years garnering the technical knowledge needed to be a trader or investor, this would ultimately be worth very little without the right psychological mindset in place.

The quotes and sayings posted on Twitter were making my clients better traders; inspiring them to think and act differently to achieve better results. So why not share those messages with all the traders and investors out there? I decided to set about collating all the famous (and not so famous) quotes into a book, relating each one to a specific area of trading and investing.

The world of quotes, proverbs, sayings, idioms and mottos

They seem to be everywhere these days. You can't escape them. Where do they come from though? Their sources are endless: from the ancient civilisations and culture of Greece and China - to poetry, music and literature, television commercials, business, celebrity, films, sport, current affairs and politics.

Wiktionary (the free online dictionary) gives the following definitions:

Proverbs: A short expression of popular wisdom. The wisdom is in the form of a general observation about the world or a bit of advice, sometimes more nearly an attitude toward a situation.

Quotes: To repeat or copy (words from a source such as a book), usually with acknowledgment of the source, as by way of authority or illustration. vb. esp. as a means of illustrating or supporting a statement.

Sayings: A proverb or maxim; something often said.

Mottos: A sentence, phrase, or word, prefixed to an essay, discourse, chapter, canto, or the like, suggestive of its subject matter; a short, suggestive expression of a guiding principle; a maxim.

Idiom: A common word or phrase with a culturally understood meaning that differs from what its composite words' denotations would suggest.

These definitions have changed historically over time and are often used interchangeably. For the purposes of this book, I may sometimes simply refer to them as quotes, but this should be taken to mean any of the above.

Why use quotes?

In today's fast paced, technological, media savvy world, quotes can have a huge impact and influence in supporting and promoting changes in consumerism, politics, religion, business and society.

More importantly, to the individual they can be used as a self-affirmation tool. They can be used to inspire, motivate and stimulate thinking, to help a person achieve their goals or to think differently about how they want to lead their life.

The beauty of quotes, is that once translated from their origin, they can be utilised by any culture or individual and transcend race, politics, religion and nation. They are, in fact, a very powerful tool and play a very important part in the world of psychology and human performance.

To some they may appear 'tacky' or 'cheesy', but they do work. They do make you stop and think. They can purify and simplify our thought processes and alter them, so we can believe that nothing is impossible. They can make you act differently. They can, in just a few simple words, convey such a powerful message that they can change your life!

Chinese fortune cookies

Not a pure Chinese invention at all – more an American and Chinese 20th century amalgamation. What are they? A simple cookie with a piece of paper inside. On that paper is your 'fortune' given as an aphorism; a saying or observation expressing a general truth or principle and presented in a concise statement.

The fortune cookie may have been your introduction to the world of proverbs and sayings in your childhood and cemented the idea of the importance of the quote at an early stage in your development.

Over 3 billion fortune cookies are made each year globally, so the cookies' messages reach a big audience! Nearly half of those are produced by one company: Wonton Food Inc of New York, so the sayings they use are more than likely to be found with your Chinese meal. Some of the more popular sayings I found[9] that I thought could relate to your trading and investing are:

"You will find a bushel of money"
"Don't panic"
"Okay to look at past and future. Just don't stare."
"Avert misunderstanding by calm, poise, and balance."
"Do you believe? Endurance and persistence will be rewarded."
"One that would have the fruit must climb the tree"
"People learn little from success, but much from failure."

"I hear and I forget. I see and I remember. I do and I understand."

These are obviously meant to be light hearted in nature and probably thrown away with the leftovers, but they do serve a serious point. The point being, that we do take notice of the wisdom and experience of others to formulate our own life plans and goals, however much we think we don't.

WHO IS THIS BOOK FOR?

Quite simply, it is for those who want to improve and take their trading and investing to the next level. It is for those who appreciate that there is more to successful trading and investing than just hitting the buy and sell buttons and crossing their fingers.

It is for the part-timer, the hobbyist, the new trader, the experienced investor or professional trader. In my experience, you can never stop learning and developing, however much you think you know already, and this book may just motivate and inspire you to greater success.

In both the amateur and professional sphere of trading and investing, there is a very fine line between success and failure. So, what is it that makes the winners successful? What is the edge that makes all the difference?

I believe it all comes down to having the right mindset. You can be given all the best tools, education and resources, but if you don't have the right mindset in place to take advantage of them and you can't cope with the pressures, randomness and peculiarities of the financial markets and its participants, then you're finished before you've even started.

Psychological studies have shown that harnessing positive emotions can seriously improve your performance and results in all aspects of life, not only in your trading and investing. A simple proverb or quote can be used as a tool of positivity and inspiration to enhance your attitude and behaviours to produce favourable outcomes.

Understanding and using the power of the proverb in your trading and investing may just bring you the rewards you seek.

HOW THIS BOOK WORKS

The book is broken down into six key parts:

#TRADINGJOURNEY looks at learning and you. Gaining the right knowledge, education and experiences is critical to your trading journey, but the biggest factor in your trading journey that is also one of the most overlooked, is you!

#TRADINGDISASTER when it all goes wrong it can go wrong very quickly! Most disaster is brought on by two words: fear and greed and mostly by you! This part also addresses some of the deadly sins around ego, mistakes, gossip, gambling and luck and concludes with a look at failure.

#TRADINGMINDSET looks at the fundamental approach and key personality traits required to stave off disaster and improve your results. It also looks at the mindset you need to think like a winner.

#TRADINGSKILLS it's no good playing the game if you don't know its rules, peculiarities and nuances. This part looks at the vital skills you need to give you the edge and stay in for the long term.

#TRADINGGURUS when the masters of the dark art speak, you should listen and learn. This part contains a collection of valuable quotes from some of the best in the business.

#TRADINGWISDOM passed down from the ancients, in some cases thousands of years ago, these proverbs, sayings and quotes have stood the test of time and are still relevant to the success of your trading and investing today.

Each part aims to inspire or motivate you into some sort of action. They are simply laid out with a brief explanation (where necessary) of the trading concept, followed by quotes that are related to it.

You should think hard about each of the sayings; digesting what they mean and how they relate to your own trading and investing, as they can be interpreted in many ways.

There is a basic three step common sense process to apply when utilising the quotes in the book:

1. **STOP**
2. **THINK**
3. **ACTION**

STOP and take your time to digest the saying. **THINK** how it impacts your world. Then take **ACTION** - do something. Formulate a plan as to how that quote can be applied to your trading and investing.

There is a trading saying that goes:

"You can give 100 analysts the same chart and they'll give you 100 different answers."

The same is true for these quotes and proverbs.

What makes the human race unique is its individualism. Interpretation here, is down to the individual. All I have done is steer you in the right direction, within the world of trading and investing.

Once immersed in one of the six key sections, you may recognise weaknesses and flaws in your trading that need to be addressed. You may also gain some positive insights and motivations from the vast database of psychological wisdom presented here.

If mindset is the most important aspect of trading, is it ever possible to evolve into a successful trader or are you simply born to trade? Who is the ideal trader or investor and are they the same thing? The final chapter of the book concludes with a look at positive emotion and how you can utilise the power of the proverb to achieve trading and investing glory.

The Chinese philosopher Lau Tzu once said:

"The journey of a thousand miles begins with a single step."

So, let's take the first step……..

TIP: Keep a notepad handy to jot down any quotes or sayings that immediately strike you as important to your trading and investing.

#TRADINGJOURNEY
PART 1

#TRADINGTHOUGHT

"Observation, experience, memory & mathematics – these are what the successful trader must depend on." **Jesse Livermore**

Jesse Livermore, one of the most famous traders of all time, imparted an incredible amount of his own personal trading knowledge for our benefit. His trading journey in the early 1900's was famously laid out in the book "Reminiscences of a Stock Operator" and his quote above still holds very true today.

I have updated that #TradingThought for this book and categorised it into more generic headings; quite simply, Learning and You. Learning encapsulates knowledge, education and the experiences you build along your journey.

Jesse Livermore was also quoted as saying:

"A stock operator has to fight a lot of expensive enemies within himself" **Jesse Livermore**

So, the other major and often neglected factor in your trading journey, is in fact you! Sun Tzu, a famous Chinese General and philosopher dating back over 2,500 years said:

"If you know the enemy & know yourself you need not fear the results of a hundred battles." **Sun Tzu**

It is very important and critical for your trading success that you obtain the right skill set to trade the markets but also, you must have a detailed understanding of yourself.

LEARNING

Knowledge

As Gordon Gekko, in the film Wall Street[1] once said:

"The most valuable commodity I know of is information"

For the purposes of this book, we take that to mean having a full understanding of what you are trading and how you trade it (within the laws of the land!) and having a full understanding of yourself. Always look to gain knowledge.

"Knowledge is power only if man knows what facts not to bother with" **Robert Staughton Lynd**

"An investment in knowledge pays the best interest." **Benjamin Franklin**

"Real knowledge is to know the extent of one's ignorance." **Confucius**

> **Risk comes from not knowing what you're doing** *Warren Buffett*

"The best advice I ever got was that knowledge is power and to keep reading." **David Bailey**

"Knowledge of what is does not open the door directly to what should be." **Albert Einstein**

"The true method of knowledge is experiment." **William Blake**

"Knowing others is wisdom, knowing yourself is Enlightenment." **Lao Tzu**

Education

#TRADINGTHOUGHT

"Ignorance is the curse of God; knowledge is the wing wherewith we fly to heaven"
William Shakespeare

An important factor in enhancing your trading journey is getting the right education in the first place. It is also the case that, like with most things, you should never stop learning and developing and evolving. Education should always play a part in your trading journey.

"If you hold a cat by the tail you learn things you cannot learn any other way." **Mark Twain**

"I never let school interfere with my education." **Mark Twain**

"Untutored courage is useless in the face of educated bullets." **George S Patton**

> ❝ Formal education makes you a living; self-education makes you a fortune. ❞ *Jim Rohn*

"Education is the most powerful weapon which you can use to change the world." **Nelson Mandela**

"The whole purpose of education is to turn mirrors into windows." **Sydney J. Harris**

"The great aim of education is not knowledge but action." **Herbert Spencer**

> Give a man a fish and you feed him for a day; teach a man to fish and you feed him for a lifetime. **Maimonides**

"To the uneducated, an A is just three sticks." **A. A. Milne**

"Education is freedom." **Paulo Freire**

"I cannot live without books." **Thomas Jefferson**

"The roots of education are bitter, but the fruit is sweet." **Aristotle**

"Books are a uniquely portable magic." **Stephen King**

"The man who does not read good books has no advantage over the man who cannot read them." **Mark Twain**

Experience

You can't buy it! It will give you the insights and skills that can't be learnt from books, YouTube videos or on a course. You must 'live' trading to get a feel for it. If you don't get the right and necessary experiences, you will fail. You should keep learning, keep practising and roll with the punches if you're ever going to make it as a trader.

"If the facts don't fit the theory, change the facts." **Albert Einstein**

> **Practice puts brains in your muscles.**
> *Samuel Snead*

"We are what we repeatedly do. Excellence, then, is not an act, but a habit." **Aristotle**

"An ounce of practice is generally worth more than a ton of theory." **Ernst F. Schumacher**

"Practice isn't the thing you do once you're good. It's the thing you do that makes you good." **Malcolm Gladwell**

"The only source of knowledge is experience." **Albert Einstein**

"No man ever steps in the same river twice, for it's not the same river and he's not the same man." **Heraclitus**

"Life can only be understood backwards; but it must be lived forwards." **Soren Kierkegaard**

> **Practice does not make perfect. Only perfect practice makes perfect.** *Vince Lombardi*

"You cannot create experience. You must undergo it." **Albert Cam**

"Life is the art of drawing without an eraser." **John W. Gardner**

#TRADINGTHOUGHT

"Experience is the teacher of all things." **Julius Caesar**

❛ Is there anyone so wise as to learn by the experience of others? ❜ *Voltaire*

"A man who carries a cat by the tail learns something he can learn in no other way." **Mark Twain**

"The value of experience is not in seeing much, but in seeing wisely." **William Osler**

"Skill is the unified force of experience, intellect and passion in their operation." **John Ruskin**

❛ All adventures especially into new territory are scary. ❜ *Sally Ride*

"Good judgment comes from experience, and experience comes from bad judgment." **Rita Mae Brown**

"I'd rather have a lot of talent and a little experience than a lot of experience and a little talent." **John Wooden**

"The years teach much which the days never know." **Ralph Waldo Emerson**

"Experience is simply the name we give our mistakes." ***Oscar Wilde***

"Nothing ever becomes real till it is experienced." ***John Keats***

"I go by instinct - I don't worry about experience." ***Barbra Streisand***

"Experience: that most brutal of teachers. But you learn, my God do you learn." ***William Nicholson***

YOU

You…. the most important part of the trading journey jigsaw! In my trading experience, I believe there is not a single type of trader or investor that can be marked out as a successful role model to emulate 100%. Everybody is uniquely different. However much you think you can copy them, you must be yourself.

> **One can have no smaller or greater mastery than mastery of oneself** *Leonardo da Vinci*

"Always be a first-rate version of yourself, instead of a second-rate version of somebody else." **Judy Garland**

"Know thyself." **Socrates**

Yes, you can learn from others, but at the end of the day you must develop your own style and trading personality if you are going to succeed. As in the world of sport, even team sports, it really is all about the individual - YOU.

If you don't understand yourself and how you interact with the markets, you will also become your own greatest enemy, eventually leading to total failure.

"The market does not know you exist, you can't influence it. You can only control your behaviour" **Dr. Alexander Elder**

"It is hard to fight an enemy who has outposts in your head" **Sally Kempton**

"Knowing yourself is the beginning of all wisdom." **Aristotle**

"We don't see things as they are, we see them as we are." **Anaïs Nin**

"No man ever steps in the same river twice, for it's not the same river and he's not the same man." **Heraclitus**

"It has been a motto of mine my whole life - just be yourself." **Patrick Kane**

❛ In three words, I can sum up everything I've learned about life: it goes on. ❜ Robert Frost

"If we did all the things we were capable of doing, we would literally astound ourselves." **Thomas Edison**

#TRADINGTHOUGHT
"Be yourself; everyone else is already taken." **Oscar Wilde**

#TRADINGDISASTER
PART 2

#TRADINGTHOUGHT
"The buck stops here."
Harry Truman

Trading disaster can come more quickly to some, than others. Disaster can be attributed to unexpected, unforeseen and uncontrollable events outside of the trader's control i.e. the behaviour of the market, but in reality most disaster is self-inflicted.

Individuals like to lay the blame at somebody's feet; whether it was the market, their broker or their pet cat jumping onto their computer, hitting the sell button whilst they weren't looking - they will always find an excuse. They always like to blame lady luck!

Two words capture the essence of personal, self-inflicted trading disaster: Fear and Greed.

"Fear & greed are potent motivators. When both push in the same direction, virtually no human being can resist." **Andrew Weil**

"Fear, greed, hope have destroyed more portfolio value than any recession or depression we've ever been through." **James O'Shaughnessy**

Fear and greed, by their nature, lead us to participating in destructive human actions which ultimately destroy our trading.

FEAR & GREED

Fear can strike the unprepared, uneducated, risk averse, timid and unsure. It can make you make foolish decisions, hesitate, over analyse or even paralyse your trading full stop. You listen to others' advice and gossip instead of thinking for yourself. It stops you from putting that trade on, makes you believe you'll lose out or make losses. It adds unmanageable stress to your trading.

On the flip side, there is greed. Greed is equally as dangerous. Greed can make you put aside your common sense and self-control. It introduces the ego, addiction, unfounded hope, euphoria, excitement, temptation and ignorance.

Gordon Gekko, in the film Wall Street[2] said:

"The point is ladies and gentlemen that greed, for lack of a better word, is good."

He's right to some extent, but controlled greed in trading works much better.

Both fear and greed make you make stupid mistakes. They make you lazy, cut corners, make you distracted, unfocused and undisciplined, all of which eventually result in trading disaster. This in turn, leads to feelings of failure and the desire to exact revenge. The only way to counter this is to learn how to manage fear and greed.

Fear

"Fear is a reaction. Courage is a decision." **Sir Winston Churchill**

"The oldest, strongest emotion of mankind is fear & the oldest & strongest kind of fear is fear of the unknown." **H. P. Lovecraft**

"True success is overcoming the fear of being unsuccessful." **Paul Sweeney**

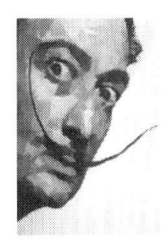

#TRADINGTHOUGHT
"Have no fear of perfection - you'll never reach it." **Salvador Dali**

"And the things that we fear are a weapon to be held against us." **Ian Rush**

"Fears are nothing more than a state of mind." **Napoleon Hill**

"To fight fear, act. To increase fear - wait, put off, postpone." **David Joseph Schwartz**

> **I'm not afraid of storms, for I'm learning how to sail my ship.** *Louisa May Alcott*

"Always do what you are afraid to do." **Ralph Waldo Emerson**

"A person's fears are lighter when the danger is at hand." **Lucius Annaeus Seneca**

> **Fear is the mother of foresight.** *Thomas Hardy*

"When you're fearful, you stumble." **Jenna Jameson**

"We fear things in proportion to our ignorance of them." **Christian Nestell Bovee**

"If you want to conquer fear, don't sit home and think about it. Go out and get busy." **Dale Carnegie**

"My motto is: feel the fear and do it anyway." **Tamara Mellon**

"Nothing in life is to be feared; only to be understood. Now is the time to understand more, so that we fear less." **Marie Curie**

> **Don't be afraid to see what you see.**
> *Ronald Reagan*

"We are afraid of the enormity of the possible." **Emile M. Cioran**

Often, fear can create paralysis in your trading and investing. It puts demons in your mind and plays on your mental weaknesses. It can stop you doing the job. The very old idiom in this case rings true:

"You can lead a horse to water, but you can't make it drink."

In trading and investing you must drink that water!

Greed

"A wiseman should have money in his head, but not in his heart" **Jonathan Swift**

"We all seem to be about aggression & greed. It's a massive pressure that affects us all." **Eric Cantona**

"The ignorant mind, with its infinite afflictions, passions, evils, is rooted in the 3 poisons: Greed, anger, delusion." **Bodhidharma**

"Greed is so destructive. It destroys everything." **Eartha Kitt**

> **I am guilty of stupidity, arrogance, and greed.**
> *Steve Madden*

"Nothing makes us more vulnerable than loneliness, except greed." **Thomas Harris**

"I'll argue that greed is a much more subtle vice than simply the desire to be rich." **Stanley Hauerwas**

DESTRUCTIVE ACTIONS

Ego

If you want to become a great trader, leave your ego at the door…

"The ego is not master in its own house." **Sigmund Freud**

"The ego is a fascinating monster." **Alanis Morissette**

"One may understand the cosmos, but never the ego; the self is more distant than any star." **Gilbert K. Chesterton**

> Avoid having your ego so close to your position that when your position falls, your ego goes with it. *Colin Powell*

"Your ego can become an obstacle to your work. If you start believing in your greatness, it is the death of your creativity." **Marina Abramovic**

"Whenever I climb I am followed by a dog called 'Ego'." **Friedrich Nietzsche**

Gossip

If it sounds or reads too good to be true, it normally is, in the world of trading. Don't be lazy; do your own leg work.

"Gossip is the Devil's radio." **George Harrison**

> If you've read it in the papers it's too late – move on, forget it. *Stephen Hoad*

"One Swallow makes ('tis true) no Summer, yet one tongue may create a rumour." *Thomas D'Urfey*

Gambling

Gamblers lose 99 times out of 100 in the long run. They are a weapon unto themselves that the casino owner or bookie loves! Successful traders are not gamblers. They are educated, controlled, calculated risk takers.

"Depend on the rabbit's foot if you will, but remember it didn't work for the rabbit." **R.E. Shay**

"I was very fortunate in my gene mix. The gambling instincts I inherited from my father were matched by my mother's gift for analysis." *T. Boone Pickens*

"Oh, it's not really gambling when you never lose." *Jennifer Aniston*

"Gambling: The sure way of getting nothing for something."
Wilson Mizner

"Uncertainty doesn't make life worth living, but it does make striving and gambling worth attempting." **Walter Kirn**

> There are many lessons to be learned from gambling; the harshest one is the difference between having fun & being Smart.

Hunter S. Thompson

"Money won is twice as sweet as money earned."[7] **From the movie, The Colour of Money**

Mistakes

It is fine to make mistakes, as long as you learn from them and don't repeat them. Don't retaliate, try to get even or revenge trade. Stay calm, focused, stick to the rules, take it on the chin and move on – think of the long game. Often, the markets won't give you a second chance; they take no prisoners and they don't care who you are.

"The greatest mistake you can make in life is to be continually fearing you will make one." **Elbert Hubbard**

"The only real mistake is the one from which we learn nothing." **John Powell**

"From the errors of others, a wise man corrects his own." **Syrus**

"Mistakes are always forgivable, if one has the courage to admit them." ***Bruce Lee***

> **The successful man will profit from his mistakes and try again in a different way.** *Dale Carnegie*

"Do not fear mistakes. You will know failure. Continue to reach out." ***Benjamin Franklin***

"Take chances, make mistakes. That's how you grow. Pain nourishes your courage. You have to fail in order to practice being brave." ***Mary Tyler Moore***

> **Mistakes are the portals of discovery.**
> ***James Joyce***

"You make mistakes. Mistakes don't make you." ***Maxwell Maltz***

Luck

Relying on, or blaming, luck is a dangerous thing in the world of trading. Yes, sometimes luck can play its part; sometimes there are just things that happen that are way out of your control. Most of the time though, your trading and the fruits of your trading don't come down to luck at all, they come down to your skill as a trader.

As they say, you make your own luck.

"Luck never gives; it only lends." ***Swedish Proverb***

"Luck is what you have left over after you give 100 percent." ***Langston Coleman***

❝ **Luck never made a man wise.** ❞ *Seneca*

"The only thing that overcomes hard luck is hard work." **Harry Golden**

"The best luck of all is the luck you make for yourself." **Douglas MacArthur**

#TRADINGTHOUGHT

"Things do not happen. Things are made to happen" **John F Kennedy**

"Diligence is the mother of good luck." **Benjamin Franklin**

"To the soldier, luck is merely another word for skill." **Patrick MacGill**

"Shallow men believe in luck. Strong men believe in cause and effect." **Ralph Waldo Emerson**

"Care and diligence bring luck." **Thomas Fuller**

"I think luck gets you on to the stage. But it has nothing to do with keeping you there." **Eric Bana**

❝ **Success is simply a matter of luck. Ask any failure.** ❞ *Earl Wilson*

"The man who has planned badly, if fortune is on his side, may have had a stroke of luck; but his plan was a bad one nonetheless." **Herodotus**

"When it comes to luck, you make your own." **Bruce Springsteen**

> If things are going untowardly one month, they are sure to mend the next. *Jane Austen.*

Failure

The general gist from the following set of quotes is that yes, failure and losses in your trading and investing can happen, but from those experiences you should take the lessons you've learned, understand them and fight harder.

"Sometimes by losing a battle you find a new way to win the war." **Donald Trump**

Real, true failure and trading oblivion, comes not from making mistakes, but from making mistakes and carrying on regardless.

"Man looks in the abyss, there's nothing staring back at him. At that moment, man finds his character." **Lou, from the movie Wall Street**[2]

"I've failed over and over and over again in my life and that is why I succeed." **Michael Jordan**

"It's fine to celebrate success but it is more important to heed the lessons of failure." **Bill Gates**

"Do not fear mistakes. You will know failure. Continue to reach out." **Benjamin Franklin**

"Indecision and delays are the parents of failure." **George Canning**

"I have not failed. I've just found 10,000 ways that won't work." **Thomas Edison**

"Failure to prepare is preparing to fail." **Mike Murdock**

> The season of failure is the best time for sowing the seeds of success.
> *Paramahansa Yogananda*

"Failure is good. It's fertilizer. Everything I've learned about coaching, I've learned from making mistakes." **Rick Pitino**

#TRADINGTHOUGHT

"Many of life's failures are suffered by those who don't realise how near they were to success when giving up." **Thomas Edison**

"There is no such thing as failure. There are only results." **Tony Robbins**

> Failure is the condiment that gives success its flavour. *Truman Capote*

Revenge

Revenge, we've all been there!

A trade you thought was a dead cert goes against you, you get taken out and you immediately place a trade in the new direction, as you can't understand why you were wrong in the first place. Then, that trade goes against you and you cut yourself out at a loss! So, two losing trades and a depleted bank balance because of your desire to get even.

Really, you need to step back, take a deep breath and start again according to your trading plan. Frank Sinatra summed it up very nicely:

"The best revenge is massive success"

You won't get massive success if you revenge trade or invest!

Others think that the market owes them. It doesn't. You can't take revenge on the market. This mindset will finish you off and very quickly.

"Don't go around saying the world owes you a living. The world owes you nothing. It was here first." **Mark Twain**

❛ Anger is a wind which blows out the lamp of the mind ❜*Robert Green Ingersoll*

Trading is about controlling your fear and greed, keeping a check on your ego, putting in the effort to make your own luck, not blaming others, taking it on the chin when you're wrong and moving on. In other words, having the right mindset.

#TRADINGMINDSET
PART 3

#TRADINGTHOUGHT

"Trading can be an emotional rollercoaster- mastering your psychology is vital to success"
Stephen Hoad

So, how do you stave off trading disaster? That, in itself is a million-dollar question! A large number of people, even in the professional world of trading, lose at this game. What you can do though, is increase your odds and chances of success by helping yourself.

It's all about survival of the mentally fittest, so you need the right mindset and approach. You need to understand the psychological field that you are playing on and learn to control your emotions.

"Successful trading is more a state of mind than a state of mechanical or cognitive understanding of the market" **David Nassar**

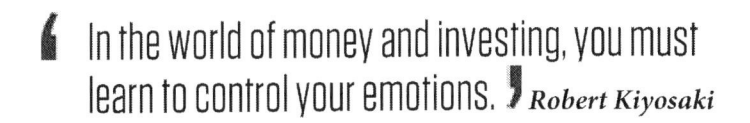

> In the world of money and investing, you must learn to control your emotions. **Robert Kiyosaki**

Academic research[5,6] has shown that positive emotions can help you to think and act smarter, even under stress. As trading and investing is inherently stressful, staying positive by having the right mindset, will only be beneficial for you.

"To create something exceptional, your mindset must be relentlessly focused on the smallest detail." **Giorgio Armani**

> **Anyone can train to be a gladiator. What marks you out is having the mindset of a champion.**
>
> *Manu Bennett*

"Success is really about your mindset." **F. Gary Gray**

"It is hard to fight an enemy who has outposts in your head" **Sally Kempton**

Part 3 starts by looking at your fundamental approach to trading and investing. What core attitudes and behaviours do you need to have in place before you start? What should your approach be?

Next, I discuss the key personality traits that are shared by the best traders and investors. What traits do they have that you may need to develop?

The last section looks at the importance of having a winning mindset. What does it feel like to win, to be successful? Thinking and acting like a winner can produce positive results and improve your future outcomes.

FUNDAMENTAL APPROACH

If you can't pull yourself out of bed on a cold, wet day, put in the extra hours and have a core level of self-motivation, then you're wasting your time. Psychologist Gordon Allport described attitudes as "the most distinctive and indispensable concept in contemporary social psychology."[13]

Attitude evolves from a person's ideas, values, beliefs, perception, family, politics, economics and society, so you can see how difficult it can be to get the 'right' attitude to trade and invest as your life has been clouded already by its past and future beliefs.

Jung's definition, in his book 'Psychological Types'[14] described attitude as "a readiness of the psyche to act or react in a certain way". If you have the right attitude, this will instill the positive motivation to react; to drive you on, to learn, develop and handle the good and bad times in your trading and investing.

"Through the mud and blood to the green fields beyond" **Irish Army Cavalry Corps**

"My motto is, 'Never quit.'" **Henry Rollins**

"Be all you can be." **United States Army motto**

"Who Dares Wins" **British Special Air Service (SAS)**

"Audere est Facere (To dare is to do)" **Tottenham Hotspur**

"For success, attitude is equally as important as ability." **Walter Scott**

#**TRADING**THOUGHT
"Attitude is a little thing that makes a big difference." **Winston Churchill**

"Between stimulus and response, there is a space where we choose our response." **Stephen Covey**

"A negative attitude is nine times more powerful than positive attitude." **Bikram Choudhury**

"Courage is what it takes to stand up and speak; courage is also what it takes to sit down and listen." **Winston Churchill**

So, let's take a look at the core attitudes and behaviours that are essential if you want to succeed.

Committed, hardworking & disciplined

The Cambridge Dictionary definition of commitment says it is:

"A willingness to give your time and energy to something that you believe in, or a promise or firm decision to do something."

Commitment and attitude go hand in hand. Lou from the film Wall Street[2] said "You can't get a little bit pregnant". It makes perfect sense doesn't it!

You'd be amazed how many individuals think they can 'buy' their way to trading success, by taking short cuts promised by unscrupulous marketers whose only aim is to part you from your money.

Throwing money at it, is really only a short-term solution. If you want to truly master trading and investing and get those results that Malcolm Gladwell describes as 'Outliers'[15] then you're only going to get that through hard work, discipline and commitment.

There are NO short cuts in life. If you want to get to the top in any endeavor, whether that be in sports, science or business, you have to commit yourself 100% if you want to succeed, master and achieve.

Putting in the hours now, will take you to that level of unconscious consciousness that will make trading and investing much easier.

"Without commitment, you cannot have depth in anything, whether it's a relationship, a business or a hobby." **Neil Strauss**

"My motto is: feel the fear and do it anyway." **Tamara Mellon**

"Do it Now!" **Napoleon Hill**

"There are only two options regarding commitment. You're either in or you're out. There's no such thing as life in-between." **Pat Riley**

"If you really want to do something, you'll find a way. If you don't, you'll find an excuse." **Jim Rohn**

> **Determination, commitment to an unrelenting pursuit of your goal-a commitment to excellence-will enable you to attain success.** *Mario Andretti*

"The only limit to your impact is your imagination and commitment." **Tony Robbins**

"The difference between involvement & commitment is like ham and eggs. The chicken is involved; the pig is committed. **Martina Navratilova**

> **Unless commitment is made, there are only promises and hopes... but no plans.** *Peter Drucker*

"No one knows what he can do until he tries." **Publilius Syrus**

"No pain, no gain." **Exercise motto**

"Per Ardua Ad Astra (Through adversity to the stars)" **Royal Air Force (United Kingdom)**

"It seems the harder I work, the more luck I have." **Thomas Jefferson**

"Only the best is good enough" **Everton Football Club**

"The dictionary is the only place that success comes before work." **Vince Lombardi**

"Discipline is the bridge between goals and accomplishment." **Jim Rohn**

"Without hard work and discipline it is difficult to be a top professional." **Jahangir Khan**

#TRADINGTHOUGHT

"Just do it!" **Nike Inc. motto**

"There is only one sort of discipline, perfect discipline." **George S. Patton**

"Most people want to avoid pain, and discipline is usually painful." **John C. Maxwell**

"If we do not discipline ourselves the world will do it for us." **William Feather**

Focused

The art of selectively concentrating on one aspect of the environment, whilst ignoring other things. Staying focused, especially for the periods of time that trading and investing can demand, can be tough. You need to be able to concentrate in the quiet times as well as during the volatile ones.

You need to be able to focus in pressure situations when the chips are down, to make the right calls. You need to constantly focus on your trading rules and objectives. If you can't concentrate and focus and you recognize this as a personal weakness, then you will need to address this problem as, being easily distracted and unfocused can be very detrimental to your trading.

To apply focus correctly, it requires you to bundle up and utilise those other skills we've already looked at: discipline, commitment, hard work and attitude.

"Focus on the journey, not the destination. Joy is found not in finishing an activity but in doing it." **Greg Anderson**

> **That's been one of my mantras - focus and simplicity.** **Steve Jobs**

"You can do anything as long as you have the passion, the drive, the focus, and the support." **Sabrina Bryan**

"We typically focus on anything that agrees with the outcome we want." **Noreena Hertz**

"One way to boost our will power and focus is to manage our distractions instead of letting them manage us." **Daniel Goleman**

"I do what I do, and I do it well, and focus and take it one moment at a time." **Jim Caviezel**

"You can't focus on other people's careers. Everybody is different." **Andy Murray**

"The more you hesitate in a game, the more your chance of getting hit. When you hesitate, usually you're in trouble." **Sidney Crosby**

"Many people don't focus enough on execution. If you commit to get something done, you need to follow through." **Kenneth Chenault**

"Realize deeply that the present moment is all you ever have. Make the Now the primary focus of your life." **Eckhart Tolle**

"Clarity affords focus." **Thomas Leonard**

"The game has its ups & downs, you can't lose focus of your individual goals" **Michael Jordan**

> One reason so few of us achieve is that we never direct our focus; Most people dabble, never deciding to master anything. *Tony Robbins*

"I'm trying to stay as calm as possible & focus. I feel everything: anxiety, excitement, nerves, pressure & joy." **Shawn Johnson**

"You can focus on things that are barriers or you can focus on scaling the wall or redefining the problem." **Tim Cook**

"Focus is a matter of deciding what things you're not going to do." **John Carmack**

"The focus should not be on talking. Talk is cheap. It must be on action." **Howard Berman**

> My greatest asset now is my focus.
> *Josh McDowell*

Prepared

What you put in is what you'll get out. Being prepared for as many of trading and investing's eventualities as you can, by putting in the hard work now, will put you in a better place when the chips are down. Equally, it will allow you to take advantage of situations in your trading and investing that you'd otherwise have failed in or struggled to deal with. So be prepared.

"Spectacular achievement is always preceded by unspectacular preparation." **Robert H Schuller**

"Be prepared." ***Motto of the scouting movement - created by Robert Baden-Powell***

"By failing to prepare, you are preparing to fail." ***Benjamin Franklin***

"Men succeed when they realize that their failures are the preparation for their victories." ***Ralph Waldo Emerson***

> **There are no secrets to success. It is the result of preparation, hard work, and learning from failure.** *Colin Powell*

"One important key to success is self-confidence. An important key to self-confidence is preparation." ***Arthur Ashe***

"Success is where preparation and opportunity meet." ***Bobby Unser***

"Success depends upon previous preparation, and without such preparation there is sure to be failure." **Confucius**

> **Luck is where opportunity meets preparation.**
> *Seneca*

Analytical

Being analytical doesn't just mean you have the ability to process numbers. In trading, it takes many forms: analysis of the markets, the fundamentals, the technicals, your results, your emotions and the emotions of others, and gauging sentiment. Beware though, there is the danger of becoming over analytical and creating the phenomenon known as paralysis by analysis!

"The ultimate authority must always rest with the individual's own reason and critical analysis." **Dalai Lama**

"To me, error analysis is the sweet spot for improvement." **Donald Norman**

"There is a syndrome in sports called 'paralysis by analysis.'" **Arthur Ashe**

"Get the habit of analysis - analysis will in time enable synthesis to become your habit of mind." **Frank Lloyd Wright**

Imaginative

A little bit of imagination can go a long way. Creative solutions around your trading can be very useful. Whether it be a new stop loss method or discovering a behavioural strategy on RBOB

Gasoline or a great way to systematise a certain market, a bit of trading dreaming won't hurt.

"Impossible is nothing" **Adidas**

"Believe you can and you're halfway there." **Theodore Roosevelt**

"Logic will get you from A to B. Imagination will take you everywhere." **Albert Einstein**

"The man who has no imagination has no wings." **Muhammad Ali**

"If you can imagine it, you can achieve it. If you can dream it, you can become it." **William Arthur Ward**

"Bring ideas in and entertain them royally, for one of them may be the king." **Mark Van Doren**

> ❝ Imagination rules the world. ❞
> *Napoleon Bonaparte*

"Imagination creates reality." **Richard Wagner**

"I saw the angel in the marble and carved until I set him free." **Michelangelo**

Passionate

By definition, passion means a powerful or compelling emotion or feeling. Although being able to control your emotions is critical for success when trading and investing having that underlying desire to achieve, to be curious, to learn and drive yourself can also be vitally as important. Having a passionate interest in the markets will be what sustains you when the going gets tough.

"I have no special talent. I am only passionately curious." ***Albert Einstein***

"If passion drives you, let reason hold the reins." ***Benjamin Franklin***

"Passion, though a bad regulator, is a powerful spring." ***Ralph Waldo Emerson***

"Never let your persistence and passion turn into stubbornness and ignorance." ***Anthony J. D'Angelo***

> Live with passion! *Tony Robbins*

PERSONALITY TRAITS

With the right fundamental approach in place, you now need to develop the personality traits that the experts say make up the best traders. You'll need to have composure, resilience, positivity, perseverance, adaptability, confidence, patience, caution, coolness, tenacity and rationality. On top of this you need to be a smart thinker, measured risk taker and psychopath. Not much then!

There is no such thing as a typical trader. Different types of trader can require different personalities. Certain markets suit certain personalities. Everybody is unique and different and brings different traits to the table. You can be a blend of some or many of the above. At the end of the day you are measured on your results!

If that list sounds intimidating or you feel there could be some chink in your trading psychological make up then you'll probably need, like any athlete needs to improve their physical fitness, to undertake your own trading mind fitness regime.

Trading mind fitness, also known as trading mindfulness, is simply examining those key components that create your trading world and looking for ways to improve them to hopefully, in turn, improve your results. In the business world you would undertake a SWOT (Strengths, Weaknesses, Opportunities and Threats) analysis to improve the business; the same goes for your own trading.

You need to conduct your own personal psychological SWOT analysis to find out what your weaknesses are, the threats your personality creates and then try to turn these into opportunities and strengths.

The following key traits that you could learn and look to adopt, are recognized as important to trading and investing success.

Composure

Emotions can be a dangerous weapon in the world of trading. You must have control and understand your emotions and the emotions and behaviour of other market participants to be a success; similar to a game of poker.

"Either you run the day, or the day runs you." **Jim Rohn**

"Too much emotion is like none at all." **Du Mu**

"If you don't manage your emotions, then your emotions will manage you." **Doc Childre and Deborah Rozman**

"Feelings are much like waves, we can't stop them from coming but we can choose which one to surf." **Jonatan Mårtensson**

> **Anger has a way of seeping into every other emotion and planting itself in there.**
> *Dane Cook*

"I am not fearless. I get scared plenty. But I have also learned how to channel that emotion to sharpen me." **Bear Grylls**

"Fear is a very explosive emotion, but it has a short life span. It's the sprint. The marathon is hope." **Mike Huckabee**

"Logic will never change emotion or perception." **Edward de Bono**

> **Only you can control your future.** Dr. *Seuss*

"When we direct our thoughts properly, we can control our emotions." **W. Clement Stone**

"I cannot always control what goes on outside. But I can always control what goes on inside." **Wayne Dyer**

Resilience:

It's about how you bounce back from loss, defeat and upset. How you deal with pressure. Jamais Cascio sums it up nicely...

"Resilience is all about being able to overcome the unexpected. Sustainability is about survival. The goal of resilience is to thrive."

Resilience gives you the psychological strength to cope. Hardship, upset, disappointment, setback will all at some time or another hit you squarely on the jaw in your life as a trader or investor. Individuals who can demonstrate resilience are people with a positive, optimistic emotional attitude and are more able in practice to balance negative and positive emotions.[16]

If you can keep a cool head when all around you are falling to pieces, then you have resilience. It's the 'rabbit in the headlights' mindset you want to avoid! Hiding or ignoring your investing or trading problems will only find you out. You have to have the resilience to deal with them. It is those who can cope in these situations that will prove out to be the winners and possibly become even stronger individuals from their experiences.

Resilience can be something you are born with or learned.[17]

"Obstacles, of course, are developmentally necessary: they teach strategy, patience, critical thinking, resilience and resourcefulness." **Naomi Wolf**

"He's a million rubber bands in his resilience." **Alan K. Simpson**

"Resilience is accepting your new reality, even if it's less good than the one you had before." **Elizabeth Edwards**

"In football, as in politics, resilience pays off." **George Osborne**

"We are all different. There is no such thing as a standard or run-of-the-mill human being, but we share the same human spirit." **Stephen Hawking**

"Man, never made any material as resilient as the human spirit." **Bernard Williams**

"Difficulties are meant to rouse, not discourage. The human spirit is to grow strong by conflict." **William Ellery Channing**

"To fly we have to have resistance." **Maya Lin**

"I assess the power of a will by how much resistance, pain, torture it endures and knows how to turn to its advantage." **Friedrich Nietzsche**

Positivity

#TRADINGTHOUGHT

"Courage is resistance to fear, mastery of fear, not absence of fear." **Mark Twain**

Positivity and optimism, are crucial traits to hold on to and very necessary in this environment. 'Positivity' is a new branch of psychology [18] and is used to 'aid understanding and the effective intervention for the achievement of a satisfactory life and personal growth.'

Improvements in positivity have been shown to come from family, social networks, clubs, organisations, physical exercise and increased personal wealth. Neuroscientific studies have also shown the benefits of being positive. [19]

Positive emotions can include excitement, satisfaction, pride and accomplishments and are heavily connected to a longer, healthier life. [18]

Trading and investing can be tough and deal you some pretty psychological as well as financial hard knocks, but if you can have a positive mindset, this will hold you in good stead. If you haven't, you need to change your negative style of thinking. Don't worry if you can't change it yourself, it can be coached.

"Every time I step out on that field, I'm 100 percent." **Robert Griffin III**

"The way to get started is to quit talking and begin doing." **Walt Disney**

"In order to carry a positive action, we must develop here a positive vision." **Dalai Lama**

"Yesterday is not ours to recover, but tomorrow is ours to win or lose." **Lyndon B. Johnson**

"If you're not making mistakes, then you're not doing anything. I'm positive that a doer makes mistakes." **John Wooden**

❝ I think anything is possible if you have the mindset and the will and desire to do it and put the time in. ❞ Roger Clemens

"It's a wonderful thing to be optimistic. It keeps you healthy and it keeps you resilient." **Daniel Kahneman**

"Always turn a negative situation into a positive situation." **Michael Jordan**

"Winners make a habit of manufacturing their own positive expectations in advance of the event." **Brian Tracy**

❝ Never stop investing. Never stop improving. Never stop doing something new. ❞

Bob Parsons

"Optimists are nostalgic about the future." **Chicago Tribune**

"It doesn't hurt to be optimistic. You can always cry later."
Lucimar Santos de Lima

"Perpetual optimism is a force multiplier." **Colin Powell**

> **My dear friend, clear your mind of can't.**
> *Samuel Johnson*

"Optimism is essential to achievement and it is also the foundation of courage and true progress." **Nicholas M. Butler**

Perseverance

Grit, determination and perseverance are essential for those tough times that WILL happen…

"That which does not kill us makes us stronger." **Friedrich Nietzsche**

"Never give up, for that is just the place and time that the tide will turn." **Harriet Beecher Stowe**

"A river cuts through rock, not because of its power, but because of its persistence." **James N. Watkins**

> **Diamonds are nothing more than chunks of coal that stuck to their jobs.** *Malcolm S. Forbes*

"Paralyze resistance with persistence." **Woody Hayes**

"Fall seven times, stand up eight." ***Japanese Proverb***

"Our greatest glory is not in never failing, but in rising up every time we fail." **Ralph Waldo Emerson**

"Problems are not stop signs, they are guidelines." **Robert Schuller**

"Success is no accident. It is hard work, perseverance, learning, studying, sacrifice. Most of all, a love of what you are doing or learning to do." **Pele**

> **Perseverance is the hard work you do after you get tired of doing the hard work you already did.**
> *Newt Gingrich*

"Patience and perseverance have a magical effect before which difficulties disappear and obstacles vanish." **John Quincy Adams**

"Perseverance is not a long race; it is many short races one after the other." **Walter Elliot**

"In the realm of ideas everything depends on enthusiasm. In the real world, all rests on perseverance." **Johann Wolfgang von Goethe**

"Through perseverance many people win success out of what seemed destined to be certain failure." **Benjamin Disraeli**

"Men fail much oftener from want of perseverance than from want of talent." **William Cobbett**

"Over time, grit is what separates fruitful lives from aimlessness." **John Ortberg**

Adaptability

The global financial markets can be highly volatile and very difficult to predict. At times, trading them will feel like you're riding a bucking bronco, so you must adapt and be flexible as the markets change.

It's not just a case of being able to react to a fast-changing environment. The best traders can also anticipate where the markets may be heading next and will evolve and adapt around their future perceptions.

> **Change before you have to.** *Jack Welch*

"There is nothing permanent except change." **Heraclitus**

"Change brings opportunity." **Nido Qubein**

"If we don't grow, we aren't really living." **Gail Sheehy**

"It is not the strongest that survive, nor the most intelligent, but the one most responsive to change" **Charles Darwin**

"People are always looking for the single magic bullet that will totally change everything. There is no single magic bullet." **Temple Grandin**

"To improve is to change; to be perfect is to change often." **Winston Churchill**

"The first step toward change is awareness. The second step is acceptance." **Nathaniel Branden**

"You must welcome change as the rule but not as your ruler."
Denis Waitley

"When the winds of change blow, some people build walls and others build windmills." **Chinese Proverb**

"There are three constants in life... change, choice and principles."
Stephen Covey

> **#TRADING**THOUGHT
> *"Change is inevitable. Change is constant."*
> **Benjamin Disraeli**

"Failure is not fatal, but failure to change might be." **John Wooden**

"You must always be able to predict what's next and then have the flexibility to evolve." **Marc Benioff**

> ❝ When one door closes, another opens ❞
> *Alexander Graham Bell*

Confidence

A trader without any confidence is a dead duck in the water! You must have confidence in yourself and what you are doing if you are going to make a success of this game.

"Life begins at the end of your comfort zone." **Neale Donald Walsch**

Often, confidence in trading and investing comes down to having the right education and experiences under your belt, so when the worst happens you'll know how to deal with it.

"Make the most of yourself, for that is all there is of you." **Ralph Waldo Emerson**

> **You have to expect things of yourself before you can do them.** *Michael Jordan*

"Confidence is preparation. Everything else is beyond your control." **Richard Kline**

"If we all did the things we are capable of doing, we would literally astound ourselves." **Thomas Edison**

"When you have confidence, you can have a lot of fun. And when you have fun, you can do amazing things." **Joe Namath**

"The most beautiful thing you can wear is confidence." **Blake Lively**

> **Confidence is contagious. So is lack of confidence.** *Vince Lombardi*

"My confidence comes from the daily grind - training my butt off day in and day out." **Hope Solo**

"Concentration, Confidence, Competitive urge, Capacity for enjoyment." **Arnold Palmer**

"Confidence comes from discipline and training." **Robert Kiyosaki**

Patience

An extremely difficult skill to master in the world of trading. Do you take your profits now, cut your losses, jump on that trade idea or wait for it to come back to you? These are just some of the questions you may face.

The markets may rattle on like a high-speed locomotive, but the best traders can take a step back when necessary and are able to patiently lay in wait for the right conditions to evolve, so that they can spring their trade to the optimal effect. Patience is a critical skill to have for longer term success.

"A handful of patience is worth a bushel of brains" **Dutch Proverb**

"Have patience. All things are difficult before they become easy." **Saadi of Shiraz**

"The strongest of all warriors are these two—Time and Patience." **Leo Tolstoy**

"Have patience with all things, but, first of all with yourself." **Saint Francis de Sales**

"Trees that are slow to grow bear the best fruit." **Moliere**

> Ambition is the path to success. Persistence is the vehicle you arrive in. **Bill Bradley**

Caution

Caution is a double-edged sword. Being too cautious can be very destructive – you may fail to put that trade on, be paralysed by your analysis, always waiting for that right moment. However, showing no caution i.e. the gambler who throws his whole hand in on red 13, is equally as dangerous. It is a fine balance to master, but a necessary one.

"The cautious seldom err." **Confucius**

> The policy of being too cautious is the greatest risk of all. *Jawaharlal Nehru*

Coolness

Handling stress, rolling with the punches and dealing with pressure when the going gets tough is all very hard to maintain over the longer term and can become soul destroying.

You can't let it though. You may see traders on the television swearing, shouting, looking like they're about to physically explode but under all that bravado is a very composed person knowing exactly what they want to do and how they'll act next.

You don't have to be an 'iceman' but certainly keeping your cool, handling the pressure and not being hot headed will all help your cause.

"He who keeps his cool best wins." **Norman Cousins**

"I just tried to keep my cool and continue with my race plan: to win." **Mark Spitz**

"Every great player has learned the two Cs: how to concentrate and how to maintain composure." **Byron Nelson**

Consistency

It's a buzz word in the field of sports and it should be in your trading and investing as well. If you want to make a long-term success out of trading and investing, being consistent is key. The best traders will churn out result after result almost in robotic fashion….

> Everything you need to get that relaxed driving that brings consistency only comes with practice. *John Surtees*

"For changes to be of any true value, they've got to be lasting and consistent." **Tony Robbins**

"Most players in this league say they want consistency." **Isaiah Thomas**

"Take control of your consistent emotions and begin to consciously and deliberately reshape your daily experience of life". **Tony Robbins**

> The secret to winning is constant, consistent management. *Tom Landry*

"Success is more a function of consistent common sense than it is of genius." **An Wang**

"To be a consistent winner means preparing not just one day, one month or even one year - but for a lifetime." **Bill Rodgers**

Tenacity

Being willful but not obstinate. Being determined and dogged but not pig-headed. Like being cautious, being tenacious or stubborn also holds a fine line between being a destructive force or one that will aid your investing. As Willie Aames says below....

"Being stubborn can be a good thing. Being stubborn can be a bad thing. It just depends on how you use it." **Willie Aames**

#TRADINGTHOUGHT
"I can take it. The tougher it gets; the cooler I get."
Richard M. Nixon[20]

"As the facts change, change your thesis. Don't be a stubborn mule, or you'll get killed." **Barry Sternlicht**

❝ They say that I'm stubborn, and my wife says that, too, but it's paid off so far. ❞
Sugar Ray Leonard

"You need to be curious, competitive, creative, stubborn, self-confident, skeptical, patient and be lucky to win a Nobel." *Ivar Giaever*

Rationality

You need to be lucid, balanced, logical and realistic. Obvious really!

"Rational beliefs bring us closer to getting good results in the real world." *Albert Ellis*

"The great advantage of being human is that we can employ rational thought and resolve to change our circumstances." *Mariella Frostrup*

"Reason: The arithmetic of the emotions." *Elbert Hubbard,*

> **Human beings lose their logic in their vindictiveness.** *Elizabeth Cady Stanton*

Smart thinking & creativity

What is smart thinking? Just because you may be intelligent doesn't necessarily mean that you'll think smart. Smart thinking allows you to think outside the box in an entrepreneurial way to come up with strategies, new trading ideas, to analyse the markets differently, help you solve problems and get things done! It is the ability to solve new problems using your current knowledge and experiences.

> **Think Different** *Apple Inc*

Smart Thinking is definitely a skill you can develop and work on. Successful traders who are smart thinkers are very good at:

- Developing smart habits.
- Acquiring high quality knowledge.
- Applying that knowledge.

"Behavioral psychology is the science of pulling habits out of rats." **Douglas Busch**

"New beginnings are often disguised as painful endings." **Lao Tzu**

"Perception is a clash of mind & eye, the eye believing what it sees, the mind seeing what it believes." **Robert Brault**

> **Success is a lousy teacher. It seduces smart people into thinking they can't lose.** *Bill Gates*

"Whatever you do in life, surround yourself with smart people who'll argue with you." **John Wooden**

"Working hard and working smart sometimes can be two different things." **Byron Dorgan**

"A smart man makes a mistake, learns from it, never makes that mistake again. A wise man finds a smart man, learns from him how to avoid the mistake altogether." **Roy H. Williams**

> **A man must be big enough to admit his mistakes, smart enough to profit from them, strong enough to correct them.** *John C. Maxwell*

"Half of being smart is knowing what you are dumb about." **Solomon Short**

"Being aware of your fear is smart. Overcoming it is the mark of a successful person." **Seth Godin**

"A smart man only believes half of what he hears, a wise man knows which half." **Jeff Cooper**

"It's better to get smart than to get mad." **John H. Johnson**

"I like to think of the world as a casino, except the house doesn't have the edge. If you're smart, you have an edge. It behooves you to place a lot of bets." **Evan Williams**

> **Smart people are a dime a dozen. What matters is the ability to think different... to think out of the box.** *Walter Isaacson*

"There are many harsh lessons to be learned from the gambling experience, but the harshest one of all is the difference between having Fun and being Smart." **Hunter S. Thompson**

Creativity also belongs in the world of the smart thinker…

"You cannot discover new oceans unless you have the courage to lose sight of the shore." **André Gide**

"Money never starts an idea. It is always the idea that starts the money." **Owen Laughlin**

"Ideas pull the trigger, but instinct loads the gun." **Don Marquis**

Measured risk taking

Risk taking, is what trading and investing is all about. It is the potential to gain or lose something of value [21] and the interaction with uncertainty. High returns go hand in hand with the level of risk you are exposed to. So, you need to take some!

Risk perception is a very subjective individual judgement process and can be completely different from one person to the next. How you manage and behave as a risk taker will determine your success though. Trading and investing has two risk taking human failures. They are located at either end of the risk-taking spectrum – the pure gambler and the completely risk averse. Both will be losers.

Both are inconsistent; one a loose cannon, the other a shrinking violet. The best traders fit somewhere in the middle. They can veer toward either ends of the poles but if they do, they will need to understand who they are in terms of their risk-taking abilities and how that fits into their trading plan.

"If everything seems under control, you're just not going fast enough." *Mario Andretti*

❝ The policy of being too cautious is the greatest risk of all. ❞ *J. Nehru*

"Living at risk is jumping off the cliff and building your wings on the way down." **Ray Bradbury**

"Risk isn't a word in my vocabulary." It's my very existence. **Slash**

"It's risky in a marriage for a man to come home too late, but it can sometimes pose an even greater risk if he comes home too early." **Marcel Achard**

> Almost everything worthwhile carries with it some sort of risk. **Chris Hadfield**

"You take unacceptable risk, you have to be prepared to face the consequence." **Carly Fiorina**

"I think there's a difference between a gamble and a calculated risk." **Edmund H. North**

"Life, like poker has an element of risk. It shouldn't be avoided. It should be faced." **Edward Norton**

"Between calculated risk and reckless decision-making lies the dividing line between profit and loss." **Charles Duhigg**

> All of life is the exercise of risk. **William Sloane Coffin**

"Yes, risk taking is inherently failure-prone. Otherwise, it would be called sure-thing-taking." **Tim McMahon**

"To eat an egg, you must break the shell." **Jamaican Proverb**

"Behold the turtle. He makes progress only when he sticks his neck out." **James Bryant Conant**

"A ship is safe in harbour, but that's not what ships are for." **William G.T. Shedd**

#TRADINGTHOUGHT

"Whatever you are, be a good one."
Abraham Lincoln

"There is no more miserable human being than one in whom nothing is habitual but indecision." **William James**

"You'll always miss 100% of the shots you don't take." **Wayne Gretzky**

"Take risks: if you win, you will be happy; if you lose, you will be wise." **Unknown**

"You must lose a fly to catch a trout." **George Herbert**

"When you play it too safe, you're taking the biggest risk of your life. Time is the only wealth we're given." **Barbara Sher**

Psychopathy

No, I haven't gone off piste with this one! Psychopaths have a lot of the skills necessary to make very good traders. For peace of mind, we're not talking your run-of-the-mill mass murderer here. They are categorised as 'bad' psychopaths. Bad psychopaths can be further broken down into sub-categories again. For example, Hannibal Lecter from the film Silence of the Lambs would be a dysfunctional psychopath, whereas Gordon Gekko from the film Wall Street would be a functional psychopath.

What we're looking for is the 'good' functional psychopath – the James Bonds of this world.[3] There is a fine line between good and bad, but the traits of the good psychopath which you should try to learn and emulate are:

- They are not ruled by their emotions - they are 'ice cool'.
- They are focused when it matters – pressure doesn't exist.
- They take responsibility for their actions.
- They are great studiers in what interests them.
- They have a great self-belief.
- They know how to win.
- They 'go for it'.
- They don't make excuses.
- They do what they must do.

"I always said that if I wasn't studying psychopaths in prison, I'd do it at the stock exchange." ***Robert D. Hare***

"There are certainly more people in the business world who would score high in the psychopathic dimension than in the general population." ***Robert D. Hare***

"We are all ready to be savage in some cause. The difference between a good man and a bad one is the choice of the cause." ***William James***

> **When superior talents as intellect & psychopathic temperament coalesce in the same person, we've the best possible condition for effective genius.**
>
> *William James*

"There is nothing either good or bad but thinking makes it so."
William Shakespeare

"I am always doing that which I cannot do, in order that I may learn how to do it."
Pablo Picasso

"He who knows himself is enlightened." **Lao Tzu**

"Man's enemies are not demons, but human beings like himself."
Lao Tzu

A MINDSET FOR SUCCESS

A positive mindset has been shown to allow the individual to widen the scope of their attention and cognition and enable adaptable and creative thinking[5]. These studies[6] have shown that positive emotions encourage learning, make you more broad minded, make you more able to cope with adversity and make you more resilient, giving you in turn better coping skills and allowing you to be more proactive.

Being motivated, being positive, daring to dream are all essential, healthy requirements for the successful trader and investor to create a more productive now and future.

"The Power of Dreams" **Honda**

"To boldly go where no man has gone before."[8] ***Star Trek (TV Show)***

Sometimes we need a little 'pick me up', inspiration or helping hand to rekindle our trading and investing motivation, passions and desire.

Maybe you've hit a losing run or whatever you decide to trade, the markets do the opposite. Being motivated helps! Motivation, doesn't have to be just drawn from the negative. When you're starting your trading journey, or for that matter working your way through it, sometimes you need goals, dreams, an end game in mind, a bit of hope to inspire and fire up the imagination and your inner passions. You need to aspire to success and adopt a winning mindset.

"Motivation is what gets you started. Habit is what keeps you going." **Jim Ryun**

"Seize the day (Carpe Diem)" **Ancient Roman Proverb**

"Motivation will almost always beat mere talent." **Norman Ralph Augustine**

"The motivation is in my heart to work toward my goals and my dreams." **Nonito Donaire**

"Sometimes when you fail, it allows you the opportunity to grow more motivation and get more intense about your training." **Abby Wambach**

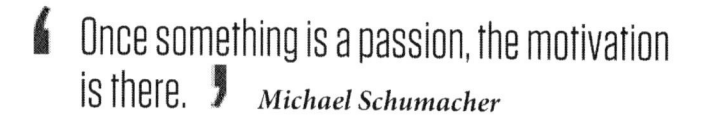

> Once something is a passion, the motivation is there. **Michael Schumacher**

"Motivation is when your dreams put on work clothes." **Unknown**

Dreams

Oneirology is the study of dreams and scientists are well aware of the importance of dreaming to human psychology and performance. Dreaming is a powerful tool that can help drive your hopes, desires, creativity and ambitions and inspire your trading and investing.

"We all have dreams. In order to make dreams come into reality, it takes a lot of determination, dedication, self-discipline, effort." **Jesse Owens**

"To accomplish great things, we must not only act, but also dream; not only plan, but also believe." **Anatole France**

"Who looks outside, dreams; who looks inside, awakes." **Carl Jung**

"Saddle your dreams before you ride em." **Mary Webb**

"Nothing happens unless first we dream." **Carl Sandburg**

Goals

If you don't have an end goal in mind, whether it be on your current trade or your plan to turn your trading into a ten-year retirement fund, then you're going to fail.

Setting goals is a fabulous process for allowing you to think about your ideal future. It is a bit different from dreaming, as in this instance you're going to take some action. Top athletes and businessmen do it and so should you.

If you know what you want to achieve, then you can organise all your time, efforts and resources into realising those goals. Goals can give you short term motivation and long term vision. Set yourself clear, precise goals. Use the SMART (Specific, Measurable, Attainable, Relevant, Time-bound) approach and live by them.

"Setting goals is the first step in turning the invisible into the visible." **Tony Robbins**

"Goals are something that can be continuously updated and should be reviewed every day – KNOW YOR GOAL. Have a plan" **Linda Bradford Raschke**

> **What keeps me going is goals** *Muhammad Ali*

"If you don't know where you are going, you will probably end up somewhere else." **Lawrence J. Peter**

"How am I going to live today in order to create the tomorrow I'm committed to?" **Tony Robbins**

"Arriving at one goal is the starting point to another." **John Dewey**

"Vision without action is a daydream. Action without vision is a nightmare." **Japanese Proverb**

> **One may miss the mark by aiming too high as too low.** *Thomas Fuller*

"Success is steady progress toward one's personal goals." **Jim Rohn**

"Review your goals twice every day in order to be focused on achieving them." **Les Brown**

"One way to keep momentum going is to have constantly greater goals." **Michael Korda**

Making Money

It's the end goal for all trading and investing activity. It's the driving reason why we do it in the first place. It's all about making money:

"The lack of money is the root of all evil." **Mark Twain**

"Money won't create success, the freedom to make it will." **Nelson Mandela**

"Money is only a tool. It will take you wherever you wish, but it will not replace you as the driver." **Ayn Rand**

> All I ask is the chance to prove that money can't make me happy. *Spike Milligan*

"Do what you love and the money will follow." **Marsha Sinetar**

"There was a time when a fool and his money were soon parted, but now it happens to everybody." **Adlai E. Stevenson**

"Sometimes your best investments are the ones you don't make." **Donald Trump**

"Real riches are the riches possessed inside." **B. C. Forbes**

"There's no such thing as a free lunch." **Milton Friedman**

"A fool and his money are soon parted." *Thomas Tusser*

#TRADINGTHOUGHT

"Pennies do not come from heaven. They have to be earned here on earth."
Margaret Thatcher

Winners

We all love winners – there is an air about them. It's the X-Factor that we crave for. Winners, live up to their potential. They achieve, they get results. They are driven and so should you be! Understanding the winner's mentality can only better your own trading and investing. It doesn't matter if they are winners in sport, business or life in general, what is important is that the success mindset can be studied, modelled, coached and utilised to your advantage.

You can reenergise yourself, creating a much more positive mindset by studying winners and what drives them to success. Learn and develop some of their characteristics and traits and add them into your trading psyche.

> **Winning is habit. Unfortunately, so is losing.**
> *Vince Lombardi*

"Winners never quit and quitters never win." **Vince Lombardi**

"Adversity causes some men to break; others to break records."
William Arthur Ward

"Most ball games are lost, not won." **Casey Stengel**

"Gold medals aren't really made of gold. They're made of sweat, determination, and a hard-to-find alloy called guts." **Dan Gable**

"We didn't lose the game; we just ran out of time." **Vince Lombardi**

> Every strike brings me closer to the next home run. **Babe Ruth**

"Life is about timing." **Carl Lewis**

"Champions keep playing until they get it right." **Billie Jean King**

"Do you know what my favorite part of the game is? The opportunity to play." **Mike Singletary**

"I won't predict anything historic. But nothing is impossible." **Michael Phelps**

"A lifetime of training for just ten seconds." **Jesse Owens**

> I'll let the racket do the talking. **John McEnroe**

"I overcame size with mechanics." **Edwin Moses**

"First, accept sadness. Realize that without losing, winning isn't so great." **Alyssa Milano**

"Winning isn't everything, it's the only thing." **Vince Lombardi**

"Winning isn't everything, but wanting it is." **Arnold Palmer**

"When you are winning a war almost everything that happens can be claimed to be right and wise." **Winston Churchill**

"Don't give up at half time. Concentrate on winning the second half." **Paul Bryant**

> Winning takes talent, to repeat takes character. **John Wooden**

"The world is won by those who let it go. But when you try and try. The world is beyond the winning." **Lao Tzu**

"It's not the winning that teaches you how to be resilient. It's the setback. It's the loss." **Beth Brooke**

"The key to winning is poise under stress." **Paul Brown**

"You learn more from losing than winning. You learn how to keep going." **Morgan Wootten**

"Winners make a habit of manufacturing their own positive expectations in advance of the event." **Brian Tracy**

> **Losers make promises they often break. Winners make commitments they always keep.** *Denis Waitley*

"There are winners, there are losers and there are people who have not yet learned how to win." **Les Brown**

"Losers live in the past. Winners learn from the past and enjoy working in the present toward the future." **Denis Waitley**

"See, winners embrace hard work." **Lou Holtz**

"Winners do what losers don't want to do." **Gary Busey**

> **One characteristic of winners is they always look upon themselves as a do it yourself project** *Denis Waitley*

"I love winners when they cry, losers when they try." **Tom T. Hall**

"No matter how long I go without riding winners, I know in the back of my head that I can ride." **Tony McCoy**

Success

Achieving success can be a long, hard road in the world of trading and investing. It can come to a point where you feel like calling it a day, but as this next batch of quotes and proverbs state, success may not be an immediate thing and must be heavily worked upon. You'll have to prepare yourself for the many setbacks you may experience before you get to the top.

"The secret to success is to do the common things uncommonly well." **John D Rockefeller Jr**

"Success comes from taking the initiative and following up." **Tony Robbins**

> You always pass failure on your way to success. **Mickey Rooney**

"There are no secrets to success. It is the result of preparation, hard work, and learning from failure." **Colin Powell**

"I don't measure a man's success by how high he climbs but how high he bounces when he hits bottom." **George S. Patton**

"3 things essential to achievement are common sense, hard work & stick-to-it-iv-ness" **Thomas Edison**

"The road to success is always under construction." **Arnold Palmer**

"Success consists of going from failure to failure without loss of enthusiasm." **Winston Churchill**

Future

If you've mapped out your goals and what you want to achieve from your trading and investing from the start, then your future is going to be an easier place to live in. If you've meshed together the correct trading mindset, know the rules of the game and are prepared for battle then you will enjoy your future much more. Dreaming helps but doing is better!

#TRADINGTHOUGHT

"The future influences the present just as much as the past."
Friedrich Nietzsche

"Even though the future seems far away, it is actually beginning right now." **Mattie Stepanek**

"The future rewards those who press on. I don't have time to feel sorry for myself. I don't have time to complain. I'm going to press on." **Barack Obama**

"The future starts today, not tomorrow." **Pope John Paul II**

"The future belongs to those who prepare for it today." **Malcolm X**

"Never let the future disturb you. You will meet it, if you have to, with the same weapons of reason which today arm you against the present." **Marcus Aurelius**

"There is nothing like a dream to create the future." **Victor Hugo**

"Tomorrow is fresh, with no mistakes in it." **L.M. Montgomery**

> It is said that the present is pregnant with the future. **Voltaire**

"Life is divided into 3 terms: that which was, which is & which will be. Let us learn from the past to profit by the present & from the present, to live better in the future." **William Wordsworth**

"Control your own destiny or someone else will." **Jack Welch**

Hope

Hope is a positive and optimistic attitude in the belief that you will achieve positive outcomes. It is a nice fluffy word. In this world though, it is like a wolf in a sheep's clothing. If you're relying on hope to succeed in trading and investing, then give up now. Hope is just as dangerous a mindset to have as that of its evil twin – luck! As we saw earlier, relying on luck will only lead to disaster.

"If you believe, you can achieve - that's my motto!" **Sophie Turner**

"Hope in reality is the worst of all evils because it prolongs the torments of man." **Friedrich Nietzsche**

"Neither should a ship rely on one small anchor, nor should life rest on a single hope." **Epictetus**

"A pessimist sees the difficulty in every opportunity; an optimist sees the opportunity in every difficulty." **Sir Winston Churchill**

> ❝ Hope is bogus emotion that only costs you money. ❞ *Jim Cramer*

"Learn from yesterday, live for today, hope for tomorrow. The important thing is not to stop questioning." *Albert Einstein*

> Change is not a destination, just as hope is not a strategy. *Rudy Giuliani*

#TRADINGSKILLS
PART 4

#TRADINGTHOUGHT

"You have to learn the rules of the game. Then you have to play better than anyone else." **Albert Einstein**

As Albert Einstein said above, you need to know the rules of the game - period. You need to have and understand the skills, tools and techniques of trading and investing if you want to be any good.

As we saw in Part3, your first goal is to put yourself in the right place mentally, to allow you to be in the right frame of mind to learn. You then have to learn the trading skills that are needed to successfully participate in the markets. However, to be able to utilise these skills effectively, you are once again dependent on your mindset.

So, the purpose of Part 4 is not to teach you the technical and practical skills you need (these can be taught on a training course), but rather to make you think why those skills are important and how to apply them to maximum effect.

Psychologically, you will find it very hard to apply and stick to the 'rules' when putting these sorts of skills into practice. Whether you've learnt these skills from a text book, a video, a training course you've been on, or you are self-taught, the mental application of them consistently is extremely difficult . You will need to master these skills not just academically, but also psychologically, if you are to become a better trader or investor.

The first section looks at general financial market and trading wisdom. Some quotes are very specific and direct, whilst others offer a more generalist opinion.

The second section looks at the 'Essential Skills' you'll need: risk management, technical anlaysis, statistics & results and strategy & planning. This is not an exhaustive skills list, as there are many other aspects to trading and investing not covered here. In my opinion though, if you want to improve your trading and investing, then this list comprises the most important aspects to get your head around.

> Psychology keeps trying to vindicate human nature. History keeps undermining the effort.

Mason Cooley

MARKET THOUGHTS

Whether you're a novice who is gaining experience from your hours spent trading, or you're already a market veteran, these quotes about the markets should resonate with you.

"It has become necessary to know how to read myself as to know how to read the tape" **Jesse Livermore**

"Falling markets are not great for your pension, but they are great for trading" **Stephen Hoad**

"Climate is what we expect, weather is what we get." **Mark Twain**

> **Markets can remain irrational longer than you can remain solvent.** *John Maynard Keynes*

"Don't throw darts at a board." **Gordon Gekko, from the film Wall Street**

"What drives financial markets at the raw basic level: the human need to feel in control" **Neo-classical behavioural finance**

"Fear tends to manifest itself more quickly than greed, so volatile markets tend to be on the downside. In up markets, volatility tends to gradually decline." **Philip Roth**

"If all the economists were laid end to end, they'd never reach a conclusion." **George Bernard Shaw**

"The man who is swimming against the stream knows the strength of it." **Woodrow Wilson**

"If in doubt stay out" **Unknown**

#**TRADING**THOUGHT

"ALWAYS stick to your trading plan, no matter what." **Stephen Hoad**

"Successful investing is anticipating the anticipations of others." **John Maynard Keynes**

"Whenever you find yourself on the side of the majority, it is time to pause and reflect." **Mark Twain**

"The first hour is the rudder of the day" ***Japanese Trading Proverb***

"You don't become expert in your field through chance and trading is no exception." **Stephen Hoad**

"Cut your losses quickly and let your profits run" **Unknown**

❝ If everyone is thinking alike, then somebody isn't thinking. ❞ George S *Patton*

"If you need a friend, get a dog." **Gordon Gekko, from the film Wall Street**

"Never argue with the tape…It's like arguing with your lungs because you have pneumonia" **Jesse Livermore**

> **The Important thing is NOT to stop Questioning** *Albert Einstein*

"Don't ask 'Can I do it' ask 'How do I do it'." **Stephen Hoad**

"If you cannot lose cheerfully do not trade in the market!" **Humphrey B Neill**

"There is only 1 side to the stock market: not the bull or the bear side but the right side." **Jesse Livermore**

> **The market does not know you exist, you can't influence it. You can only control your behaviour.** *Dr. Alexander Elder*

"One great mistake the man makes who watches the ticker all the time is that he trades too often" **William D Gann**

"Whatever happens in the stock market today has happened before and will happen again" **Jesse Livermore**

"The tape does not concern itself with the why and wherefore" **Jesse Livermore**

"A stock operator has to fight a lot of expensive enemies within himself" **Jesse Livermore**

> **Give up trying to catch the first and last eighth.** **Jesse Livermore**

"You can't depend on your eyes when your imagination is out of focus" **Mark Twain**

"In the long run, commodity prices are governed but by one law – the economic law of supply and demand" **Jesse Livermore**

"Trading the markets can be intimidating: if fear takes hold - stop, take stock & re-appraise" **Stephen Hoad**

"Prices like everything else move along the line of least resistance – they do what comes easiest" **Jesse Livermore**

ESSENTIAL SKILLS

Risk Management

Risk and trade management is a crucial skill you must learn. It will keep the shirt on your back and save you from financial ruin. Rather than being seen solely as a 'negative' tool, by gaining an understanding of risk management you can use it as a proactive tool to maximise your individual trade returns, as well the returns from your investment portfolio.

"If you don't respect risk, eventually they'll carry you out." **Larry Hite**

"It's a misconception that traders are big risk takers. They are in fact highly calculated, plan meticulously & are very consistent!" **Stephen Hoad**

> ❝ I am prepared for the worst, but hope for the best. ❞ *Benjamin Disraeli*

"You're trading on borrowed time if you don't learn how to master risk & trade management" **Stephen Hoad**

"That's the problem with money – it makes you do things you don't want to do." **Lou, from the film Wall Street**

"Amateurs want to be right. Professionals want to make money"
Unknown

> Always keep your portfolio and your risk at your own individual comfortable sleeping point. *Mario Gabelli*

"Maybe we should teach schoolchildren probability theory and investment risk management." **Andrew Lo**

"If the risk is fully aligned with your purpose and mission, then it's worth considering." **Peter Diamandis**

"Only put into your trading endeavour (whether money or time) what you are prepared to lose." **Stephen Hoad**

"The most important thing is money management, money management, money management," **Marty Schwartz**

Technical Analysis

Technical analysis, along with fundamental analysis, is one of the critical information tools to get your head around and master. In today's information age with the rapid evolvement of technology, technical analysis, or charting as it is also known, is becoming one of the tools of choice for today's investor and trader. It is a window into a particular market or asset and paints a picture for the user showing them where the asset has been, where it is now and where it could go. Some financial experts say history doesn't repeat itself and mathematicians will say price evolution should move randomly and doesn't move in trends, but the technical analyst would love to prove those critics wrong. As a tool, it works.

"History repeats itself, and repeatable cycles can be taken advantage of when trading" **Stephen Hoad**

"The trend is your friend" **Unknown**

"You can't depend on your eyes when your imagination is out of focus" **Mark Twain**

> History never really says goodbye. History says, 'See you later. *Eduardo Galeano*

"Those who do not remember the past are condemned to repeat it." **George Santayana**

"History never looks like history when you are living through it." **John W. Gardner**

"The very ink with which history is written is merely fluid prejudice." **Mark Twain**

"Memory is deceptive because it is coloured by today's events." **Albert Einstein**

"The past is really almost as much a work of the imagination as the future." **Jessamyn West**

"History is a vast early warning system." **Norman Cousins**

"A man should look for what is, and not for what he thinks should be." **Albert Einstein**

"Charting is like tracking an animal; you are looking at footprints to work out where price has been and is going" **Nicole Elliott**

#**TRADING**THOUGHT

"Who controls the past controls the future. Who controls the present controls the past." **George Orwell**

"Study history, study history. In history lies all the secrets of statecraft." **Winston Churchill**

"Time is my greatest enemy." **Evita Peron**

"The most reliable way to forecast the future is to try to understand the present." **John Naisbitt**

❝ The position size on a trade is determined by the stop. The stop is determined on a technical basis. ❞ *Bruce Kovner*

"Study the past, if you would divine the future." **Confucius**

Statistics and results

Part of the skill of becoming a better trader is to always keep on top of your results. You must record, analyse, pull to pieces the data to find out your trading and investing strengths and weaknesses. Only by doing this can you more easily optimise your trading performance. Make it part of your trading plan.

"However beautiful the strategy, you should occasionally look at the results." **Winston Churchill**

"You have to be the judge and jury of your trade results - evaluate & evolve to succeed" **Stephen Hoad**

"What we call results are beginnings" **Ralph Waldo Emerson**

"Be realistic with your returns - long term gain is better than short term bust" **Stephen Hoad**

> **Statistics are like bikinis. What they reveal is suggestive, but what they conceal is vital.**
> *Aaron Levenstein*

"Trading is a game of probability & statistics: it needn't be a casino. Play the odds. Have a plan & follow the rules" **Stephen Hoad**

"Once you replace negative thoughts with positive ones, you'll start having positive results." **Willie Nelson**

"Trading is like mastering a sport. You should constantly review your performance." **Stephen Hoad**

Strategy and Planning

It's not just a case of turning up and hitting the buy and sell buttons like a computer gamer. Successful trading requires strategy and planning and the efficient and consistent execution of those plans. You should think about and run your trading or investment portfolio like it was a business.

"Plans are nothing: Planning is everything." **Dwight D. Eisenhower.**

"I believe that people make their own luck by great preparation and good strategy." **Jack Canfield**

> All men can see these tactics whereby I conquer, but what none can see is the strategy out of which victory is evolved.
>
> *Sun Tzu*

"Sound strategy starts with having the right goal." **Michael Porter**

"Failing to plan is planning to fail." **Alan Lakein**

"I also have positive thinking. I am very constructively critical." **Valentino Rossi**

"The essence of strategy is choosing what not to do." **Michael Porter**

> Finally, strategy must have continuity. It can't be constantly reinvented.
>
> *Michael Porter*

> It's important to have a really clear strategy so when you are in business, you only have to make micro-strategy changes.

Alexa Von Tobel

"Planning is bringing the future into the present so that you can do something about it now." *Alan Lakein*

#TRADINGGURUS
PART 5

#**TRADING**THOUGHT

"If investing is entertaining & you're having fun, you're probably not making money. Good investing is boring." **George Soros**

The best of the best. These guys are legends in the field of investing and trading and their words of wisdom should be listened to.

Many of the most successful traders remain anonymous, but some do talk more than others about their trading and investing experiences such as those documented here. This gives the novice or experienced trader a crucial insight into their world, which anyone can learn from.

In the first section 'Legends' I look at some of the most prolifically vocal and globally renowned traders and investors in the world of today and yester year. They have given us a lot of free insight into what it takes to be the best and because of their popularity in this space, what they say is always well analysed and passed on to us mere mortals!

Paul Tudor Jones, founder of Tudor Investment Corporation, has his net worth in Forbes Magazine[10] in 2016 as $4.7 billion, making him the 308th richest man in the world. He is one of the most successful Hedge Fund managers in the world and a renowned expert at picking tops and bottoms in markets.

George Soros, a Hungarian by birth and chairman of Soros Fund Management and his Quantum Fund. He is known as the 'man who broke the Bank of England' when he 'shorted' the British Pound in 1992 during the black Wednesday UK currency crisis, netting him a cool $1billion! His Quantum Fund has generated $40 billion making it the most successful Hedge Fund in history. He is also known as one of the best currency speculators ever. His current net worth on the Forbes Magazine[10] Rich List in 2016 is $24.9 billion, making him the 23rd richest man in the world.

Warren Buffett, arguably one of the most successful traders and investors of all time. The third richest man in the world[10] worth $60.8 billion and chairman of Berkshire Hathaway in the US, he is nicknamed the "Sage of Omaha"[11] He is known as a 'value' investor.

Jesse Livermore, one of the all-time greats from the early part of the 20th century and known as the "Boy Plunger"[12] and the "Great bear of Wall Street". He was a stock and commodity trader who made and lost fortunes and his career is brilliantly documented in the book "Reminiscences of a Stock Operator" by Edwin Lefevre[1]. His quotes demonstrated the psychological challenges he had to deal with back then, and are still 100% relevant to your trading and investing today.

'Best of the Rest' looks at those who are also very successful traders, investors or analysts, but more unknown or less vocal. Names such as Sir John Templeton, Bruce Kovner or T. Boone Pickens.

Some of the best current batch of superstar traders don't appear here and that is because they mostly keep themselves to themselves. People like Carl Icahn, Steve Cohen, Ray Dalio, Ken Griffin. If after reading this book you do come across any words of wisdom from these sort of people, pay attention as you can only learn and benefit from what they have to say.

LEGENDS

Billionaire investors and traders who did and still do rule the roost. They didn't get to the top without knowing how to play the game, so pay attention to what they have to say.

Paul Tudor Jones

> **Don't focus on making money; focus on protecting what you have.** *Paul Tudor Jones*

"The secret to successful trading: indefatigable, undying & unquenchable thirst for information & knowledge." **Paul Tudor Jones**

"Trading requires a high degree of skill, focus, repetition. Life events, other emotional highs & lows are obstacles to success." **Paul Tudor Jones**

"At the end of the day, your job is to buy what goes up and to sell what goes down so who gives a damn about PE's?" **Paul Tudor Jones**

> **I always believe that prices move first and fundamentals come second.** *Paul Tudor Jones*

"Decrease your trading volume when you are trading poorly; increase your volume when you are trading well." **Paul Tudor Jones**
"My goal is to finish each day with more than I started."

Paul Tudor Jones

"It isn't that we had any unfair knowledge that others didn't have, it's just that we did our homework." **Paul Tudor Jones**

> **Every day I assume every position I have is wrong.** *Paul Tudor Jones*

"Where you want to be is always in control, never wishing, always trading, always first & foremost protecting your butt." **Paul Tudor Jones**

George Soros

"Volatility is greatest at turning points, diminishing as a new trend becomes established." **George Soros**

> **Markets are constantly in a state of flux. Money is made by discounting the obvious & betting on the unexpected.** *George Soros*

"Stock market bubbles don't grow out of thin air. They have a solid basis in reality, but reality as distorted by a misconception." *George Soros*

"Once we realize that imperfect understanding is the human condition there is no shame in being wrong, only in failing to correct our mistakes." **George Soros**

Warren Buffett

"We don't have to be smarter than the rest. We have to be more disciplined than the rest." **Warren Buffett**

"Wide diversification is only required when investors do not understand what they are doing." **Warren Buffett**

"Risk comes from not knowing what you're doing." **Warren Buffett,**

"The market is a device for transferring money from the impatient to the patient." **Warren Buffett**

#TRADINGTHOUGHT

"Rule No1 of investing is never lose money. Rule No2 is never forget rule No1"
Warren Buffett

"Be fearful when others are greedy. Be greedy when others are fearful." **Warren Buffett**

"Business schools reward difficult complex behaviour more than simple behaviour, but simple behaviour is more effective." **Warren Buffett**

"You don't need to be a rocket scientist. Investing isn't a game where the guy with a 160 IQ beats the guy with 130 IQ." **Warren Buffett**

"If past history was all there was to the game, the richest people would be librarians." **Warren Buffett**

"Opportunities come infrequently. When it rains gold put out a bucket not a thimble." **Warren Buffett**

Jesse Livermore

"There is only 1 side to the stock market: not the bull or the bear side but the right side." **Jesse Livermore**

"Whatever happens in the stock market today has happened before and will happen again" **Jesse Livermore**

> **The game taught me the game. And it didn't spare me rod while teaching.**
>
> *Jesse Livermore*

"The tape does not concern itself with the why and wherefore" **Jesse Livermore**

"A stock operator has to fight a lot of expensive enemies within himself" **Jesse Livermore**

"Give up trying to catch the first and last eighth." **Jesse Livermore**

"Never argue with the tape…It's like arguing with your lungs because you have pneumonia" **Jesse Livermore**

> **In the long run, commodity prices are governed but by one law – the economic law of supply and demand** — *Jesse Livermore*

"Prices like everything else move along the line of least resistance – they do what comes easiest" ***Jesse Livermore***

"It has become necessary to know how to read myself as to know how to read the tape" ***Jesse Livermore***

"Experience allows you to accumulate a lot of don'ts" ***Jesse Livermore***

> **Anticipating the market is gambling. To be patient & react only when it gives the signal is to speculate.** — *Jesse Livermore*

"Prices are never too high to start buying or too low to start selling" ***Jesse Livermore***

"There is a time to go long. There is a time to go short. There is a time to go fishing." ***Jesse Livermore***

"The obvious rarely happens, the unexpected constantly occurs." ***Jesse Livermore***

BEST OF THE REST

Not to be discounted or thought of as second class to those legends above - they simply spoke or were quoted a lot less! You should also take serious note of what these guys have to say.

"A great trader is like a great athlete. You have to have natural skills, but you have to train yourself how to use them." **Marty Schwartz**

> ❛ The most important thing about making money is not to let your losses get out of hand! ❜ **Marty Schwartz**

"There are a million ways to make money in the markets. The irony is that they're all very difficult to find." **Jack D. Schwager**

"Most investors want to do today what they should have done yesterday." **Larry Summers**

"All you need is one pattern to make a living." **Linda Raschke**

"Goals are something that can be continuously updated and should be reviewed every day – KNOW YOR GOAL. Have a plan" **Linda Bradford Raschke**

"If you cannot lose cheerfully do not trade in the market!" **Humphrey B Neill**

> **One great mistake the man makes who watches the ticker all the time is that he trades too often.** *William D Gann*

"What seems too high & risky to most generally goes higher. What seems low & cheap generally goes lower." **William O'Neil**

"I don't see markets; I see risks, rewards, and money." **Larry Hite**

"Two rules for winning in trading & life:1. If you don't bet, you can't win. 2. If you lose all your chips, you can't bet." **Larry Hite**

> **If you don't respect risk, eventually they'll carry you out.** *Larry Hite*

"If you're good, you're right 6 out of 10. You're never going to be right 9 out of 10." **Peter Lynch**

"Know what you own, and know why you own it." **Peter Lynch**

> **All the math you need in the stock market you get in the fourth grade.** *Peter Lynch*

"If most traders would learn to sit on their hands 50% of the time, they would make a lot more money." **Bill Lipschutz**

"The crowd is bargain hunting in what was; the knowing are buying what will be." ***Justin Mamis***

"I was very fortunate in my gene mix. The gambling instincts I inherited from my father were matched by my mother's gift for analysis." **T. Boone Pickens**

"In investing, what is comfortable is rarely profitable." **Robert Arnott**

❝ The four most dangerous words in investing are - This time it's different ❞ **Sir John Templeton**

"We're not going to play a winning hand every day." **John Paulson**

"Risk no more than you can afford to lose and also risk enough that a win is meaningful" **Ed Seykota**

"The elements of good trading: 1. Cutting losses, 2. Cutting losses & 3. Cutting losses." **Ed Seykota**

❝ The markets are the same now as they were 5 or 10 years ago, because they keep changing- just like they did then. ❞ **Ed Seykota**

"Win/lose, everybody gets what they want out of the market. Some people like to lose, so they win by losing money." **Ed Seykota**

"Time is your friend; impulse is your enemy." **Jack Bogle**

"The best traders have no ego. You have to swallow your pride and get out of the losses." **Tom Baldwin**

"If you personalize losses, you can't trade." **Bruce Kovner**

"I know where I'm getting out before I get in." **Bruce Kovner**

> The whole secret to winning in the stock market is to lose the least amount possible when you're wrong — *William O'Neil*

"Investing should be more like watching paint dry or watching grass grow. If you want excitement, take $800 and go to Las Vegas." **Paul Samuelson**

"In the short run, the market is a voting machine, but in the long run it is a weighing machine." **Benjamin Graham**

"Buy not on optimism, but on arithmetic." **Benjamin Graham**

> The goal of a successful trader is to make the best trades. Money is secondary.
> *Alexander Elder*

"It is essential to wait for trades with a good risk/reward ratio. Patience is a virtue for a trader." **Alexander Elder**

"The markets are unforgiving, and emotional trading always results in losses." **Alexander Elder**

"The market does not know you exist, you can't influence it. You can only control your behaviour" **Alexander Elder**

#TRADINGWISDOM
PART 6

#TRADINGTHOUGHT

"While we consider when to begin, it becomes too late." ***Japanese Proverb***

Four great, ancient civilisations and empires dating back thousands of years – the Romans, Greeks, Chinese and Japanese.

You're probably asking yourself what have they got to do with the world of trading and investing? Well, a lot more than you think. The ancient wisdom from thousands of years ago, can be very easily translated and applied to your trading today.

The way they conquered, fought, strategized and philosophised are all very useful to today's investor and trader. Although the physical challenges they faced were very different, the psychological and mental life battles they went through then, are exactly the same as those we face in our heads today. It was all about winning and losing, survival, being the fittest, smartest, sharpest, most adaptable, reactive and proactive and it is no different today.

In fact, Sun Tzu, a famous Chinese philosopher and General has had his works turned into a trading bible, inspired parts of the film Wall Street and is very popular amongst professional traders and business people alike.

JAPANESE

Japan, up until the mid-19th century, was a country very isolated from all others and deliberately so. Once they started to open up to the rest of the world, it exposed a culture, history and philosophy that was extremely rich, detailed and engrossing and extremely valuable. As time has moved on, this history has poured out from this island state for our benefit.

The Japanese invented charting techniques such as Ichimoku, Renko, Kagi and Heikin Ashi, that can seriously aid our trading. However, the underlying Japanese philosophy can also help us.

> **The first hour is the rudder of the day.**
> *Japanese Proverb*

"Fall seven times, stand up eight." ***Japanese Proverb***

"Vision without action is a daydream. Action without vision is a nightmare." ***Japanese Proverb***

"Wisdom and virtue are like the two wheels of a cart." ***Japanese Proverb***

"When the time comes, even a rat becomes a tiger." ***Japanese Proverb***

"To wait for luck is the same as waiting for death." ***Japanese Proverb***

"We learn little from victory, much from defeat." ***Japanese Proverb***

"Unless you enter the tiger's den you cannot take the cubs." ***Japanese Proverb***

"Money grows on the tree of persistence." ***Japanese Proverb***

"The crow that mimics a cormorant is drowned." ***Japanese Proverb***

> **If money be not thy servant, it will be thy master.** *Japanese Proverb*

"If you believe everything you read, better not read." ***Japanese Proverb***

"Knowledge without wisdom is a load of books on the back of an ass." ***Japanese Proverb***

CHINESE

The Chinese have a great knack of producing some legendary philosophers. Three who stand out and are especially relevant to this book are Sun Tzu, Lau Tzu and Confucius.

Sun Tzu was a great general, military strategist and philosopher from the 6th century BC and is credited as the author of the book "The Art of War", a highly influential military strategy book still used to this day. Sun Tzu's work is used heavily in the Western world, not just in the military, but also in the fields of sport, politics and business.

Lau Tzu, the founder of Taoism, was a deity and philosopher and revered in Chinese culture. It is unclear exactly when he lived, but it is presumed or argued that it was between the 6th and 4th centuries BC. His words and philosophy have a serious impact on today's society.

Confucius was a Chinese teacher, politician, deity and philosopher from between 551 to 479BC. In the world of quotes and proverbs he comes in at the top of the pile!

The final group in this section of the book are simply known as Chinese proverbs and can't be attributed to anyone but have been passed down in folklore and are widely used today and very relevant to your trading and investing.

Sun Tzu

"Invincibility lies in the defence; the possibility of victory in the attack." *Sun Tzu*

> **The important thing is victory, not persistence.** *Sun Tzu*

"He will win who knows when to fight and when not to fight." *Sun Tzu*

"The terrain or earth means to assess the situation in terms of time, distance, ease of travel and danger" *Sun Tzu*

"The good fighter should secure himself against defeat but cannot be certain of defeating the enemy" *Sun Tzu*

#TRADINGTHOUGHT

"If you know the enemy & know yourself you need not fear the results of a hundred battles." **Sun Tzu**

"Good warriors win victory by not making mistakes and positioning themselves for the win" *Sun Tzu*

"Good warriors win victory by not making mistakes and positioning themselves for the win" *Sun Tzu*

"The military has 5 rules: measurement, estimation, calculation, balancing of chances & victory" *Sun Tzu*

"As a log or stone rolls down a hill, good soldiers seek effectiveness from momentum" **Sun Tzu**

> **Warfare is fluid & changes continuously just as water will adapt its form to earth.**
> **Sun Tzu**

"A soldier's energy is at best in the morning, tiring by midday and at evening just wants to return home" **Sun Tzu**

"The general who is versatile can easily adapt and will know how to employ his forces." **Sun Tzu**

"The 5 dangerous faults in generals: carelessness, timidity, a quick temper, fragility and overconcern for troops" **Sun Tzu**

"If the enemy sees ground or position to be gained but does not act it is weak" **Sun Tzu**

"Don't attack an enemy whose ranks are in perfect order and not to advance uphill" **Sun Tzu**

> **All men can see these tactics whereby I conquer, but what none can see is the strategy out of which victory is evolved.**
> **Sun Tzu**

Lau Tzu

"New beginnings are often disguised as painful endings." **Lao Tzu**

"When you realise nothing is lacking, the whole world belongs to you." **Lao Tzu**

"By letting it go it all gets done. The world is won by those who let it go. But when you try and try. The world is beyond the winning." *Lao Tzu*

#TRADINGTHOUGHT
"A journey of a thousand miles begins with a single step." **Lau Tzu**

"If you do not change direction, you may end up where you are heading". **Lao Tzu**

"He who knows himself is enlightened." **Lao Tzu**

"Man's enemies are not demons, but human beings like himself." *Lao Tzu*

> Knowing others is wisdom, knowing yourself is Enlightenment. *Lao Tzu*

Confucius

"Real knowledge is to know the extent of one's ignorance." *Confucius*

"The will to win, the desire to succeed, the urge to reach your full potential... these are the keys that will unlock the door to personal excellence." *Confucius*

"Learning without thought is labour lost; thought without learning is perilous." *Confucius*

> By 3 methods we may learn wisdom: first, by reflection which is noblest; second, by imitation, which is the easiest; and third, by experience, which is the bitterest. *Confucius*

"A man who has committed a mistake and doesn't correct it is committing another mistake." *Confucius*

"I hear and I forget. I see and I remember. I do and I understand." *Confucius*

"When prosperity comes, do not use all of it." *Confucius*

"The essence of knowledge is, having it, to apply it; not having it, to confess your ignorance." *Confucius*

"When it is obvious that the goals cannot be reached, don't adjust the goals, adjust the action steps." *Confucius*

"A picture is a poem without words." *Confucius*

> **Not to alter one's faults is to be faulty indeed.**
Confucius

"Study the past if you would divine the future." *Confucius*

"Life is really simple, but we insist on making it complicated." *Confucius*

"It does not matter how slowly you go as long as you do not stop." *Confucius*

"Only the wisest and stupidest of men never change." *Confucius*

"To know what you know and what you do not know that is true knowledge" *Confucius*

> **Success depends upon previous preparation. Without preparation, there is sure to be failure** *Confucius*

Chinese Proverbs

"The best time to plant a tree was 20 years ago, the second-best time is now." *Chinese Proverb*

"Learning is a treasure that will follow its owner everywhere." *Chinese Proverb*

> **If you must play, decide upon three things at the start: the rules of the game, the stakes, and the quitting time.** *Chinese Proverb*

"He who asks is a fool for five minutes, but he who does not ask remains a fool forever." **Chinese Proverb**

"If you are planning for a year, sow rice; if you are planning for a decade, plant trees; if you are planning for a lifetime, educate people." **Chinese Proverb**

"If you are patient in one moment of anger, you will escape a hundred days of sorrow." **Chinese Proverb**

"When the winds of change blow, some people build walls and others build windmills." **Chinese Proverb**

"He who is not satisfied with himself will grow; he who is not sure of his own correctness will learn many things." **Chinese Proverb**

> **Teachers open the door, but you must enter by yourself.** *Chinese Proverb*

"A gem cannot be polished without friction, nor a man perfected without trials." **Chinese Proverb**

"He who could foresee affairs three days in advance would be rich for thousands of years." **Chinese Proverb**

"The one who pursues revenge should dig two graves." **Chinese Proverb**

> **Do not anxiously hope for that which is not yet come; do not vainly regret what is already past.** *Chinese Proverb*

"Small ills are the fountains of most of our groans. Men trip not on mountains, they stumble on stones." **Chinese Proverb**

"A diamond with a flaw is better than a common stone that is perfect." **Chinese Proverb**

"The journey is the reward." **Chinese Proverb**

"Learning is a treasure that will follow its owner everywhere." **Chinese Proverb**

> **If a man fools me once, shame on him. If he fools me twice, shame on me.**
> *Chinese Proverb*

"One step at a time is good walking." **Chinese Proverb**

"A single conversation with a wise man is worth a month's study of books." **Chinese Proverb**

"If we do not change our direction, we are likely to end up where we are headed." **Chinese Proverb**

"Man who waits for roast duck to fly into mouth must wait very, very long time." **Chinese proverb.**

"Patience is power; with time and patience the mulberry leaf becomes silk." **Chinese Proverb**

GREEK & ROMAN

When reading the names of the contributors in this section, it is like reading a who's who of ancient classical history – Aristotle, Julius Caesar, Socrates, Heraclitus. The Greeks and Romans, like the Chinese, have produced their own legends. They are legends of history, masters of battle, politics and philosophy. Aristotle, for example, is credited with teaching his learnings to one of the great military leaders of all time – Alexander the Great. You could do worse than to apply their wisdom to your trading and investing.

"We are what we repeatedly do. Excellence, then, is not an act, but a habit." *Aristotle*

#TRADINGTHOUGHT

"Knowing yourself is the beginning of all wisdom." **Aristotle**

"Luck is where opportunity meets preparation." ***Seneca***

"From the errors of others, a wise man corrects his own." ***Syrus***

"Experience is the teacher of all things." ***Julius Caesar***

"There is nothing permanent except change." ***Heraclitus***

"Give a man a fish and you feed him for a day; teach a man to fish and you feed him for a lifetime." **Maimonides**

"The roots of education are bitter, but the fruit is sweet." **Aristotle**

"Neither should a ship rely on one small anchor, nor should life rest on a single hope." **Epictetus**

"Never let the future disturb you. You will meet it, if you have to, with the same weapons of reason which today arm you against the present." **Marcus Aurelius**

"Know thyself." **Socrates**

"No one knows what he can do until he tries." **Publilius Syrus**

> No man ever steps in the same river twice, for it's not the same river and he's not the same man. **Heraclitus**

"More men have become great through practice than by nature." **Democritus**

FINAL THOUGHT

Who is the ideal trader or investor?

Trading and investing is a tough, hard, unforgiving master. At the end of the day, success is measured by the money you have left in your pocket. It doesn't matter how you get to the end of your journey, you just have to get there.

When you look back at sports results from 50 or 60 years ago, it is often the case you'll just read a score. You may never know whether the 1-0 football win was an easy or hard fought match, or whether during the 100 runs the batsman got in the game of cricket, he was dropped 5 times and rode his luck or he just owned it – the point is they got to the end of their journeys. The record books show them as winners.

So, who would make the ideal trader or investor? Can you bottle up their magic formula and turn yourself into a trading and investing guru? Hopefully, you will have learned from the book that there is no 'secret sauce' available anywhere, period! What you can do though is watch, study and learn from the very best.

In today's media age, there is so much information freely available for anyone to digest and learn from. Commit to learning all you can about the markets, its peculiarities, its nuances. Master the necessary tools, for example technical and fundamental analysis. You have to put in the hard work to give yourself the best chance of success. Success boils down at the end of the day to just one variable: YOU!

If we take away the pre-requisite that anyone playing this game has to have a thorough knowledge and understanding of how the markets work, technical skills and a basic but sound numerical ability, that leaves us with just the psychological makeup of the best traders. If we had to bucket what makes up the best traders, then the fundamental behaviours and personality traits we looked at in Part 3 encapsulate the ideal trader and investor from a psychological perspective.

Thomas Fuller[4] also did some great work on the trading mind set, which is summarized in the list below. According to Fuller, the ideal trader:

- Accepts the risks he takes.
- Focuses on strategy not money.
- Manages wins and losses the same, emotionally.
- Enjoys the process.
- Never feels a victim of the markets.
- Always tries to improve their skills.
- Trades completely rationally.
- Never gets angry if it isn't going well.
- Learns from their trading.
- Is not influenced by external factors.
- Is confident about their actions.
- Takes what the market offers – doesn't ring it dry.
- Trades with money they can spare.
- Takes full responsibility for all their results.
- Is relaxed during trading.
- Can focus on the present.
- Doesn't care which way the market goes.

I have worked with traders from all sorts of backgrounds from NASA scientists to Parisian mathematicians and 'barrow boys' from the East End of London. What I noticed was that they all had one thing in common – they were all themselves. They were smart thinkers. Yes, they garnered and used knowledge from the best resources, but when it came to doing the job they were very much individuals beholden to themselves. It was them who pressed the fire button, them who called the shots and them who ultimately made the decisions which lead to success or failure.

That is one of the great aspects of trading and investing. It is a great leveler. It doesn't care what your background is, where you are from or what University you went to. Trading and investing success is solely down to you. Therefore, if you don't have the right mind set in place then you are going to fail.

The 80/20 Pareto principle[22], which states that with many events roughly 80% of the effects come from 20% of the causes, is vitally important to your trading and investing journey.

If you want to become a Royal Marine, they say it is 20% physical and 80% psychological. There is a similar rule I use when trying to explain to clients what I think you need to do to become a successful trader or investor. I firmly believe, that it will take you 80% of your time to master the skills, tools and fundamentals of trading and investing but only 20% of your time to actually do it. 80% of your success will be down to your psychology and 20% to other variables. Those 20% of 'other variables' you will come to control from the 80% of time you put in to learning the game in the first place.

Are traders and investors two different types of people?

Yes and no. It is a fine line. Both camps, at the extremes, need very different mindsets to succeed. That is simply down to the nature of their jobs. However, there is a similar mentality underlying both. They must still deal with the same decisions and questions.

Often, the real big difference and the one that differentiates the two parties, is the speed with which things happen. The investor has a much longer holding time period, whereas the trader has holding periods down to the second. The trader can be more emotionally detached, use different tools to the investor and be more ruthless and aggressive, because they must be. The investor builds his portfolio over time, is more passive and is more fundamentally decision based.

At the end of the day though, their success will be measured by how much money they make and because of this, they will both share the same psychological emotions and need the same underlying mindset as each other. It is a similar scenario to the story of the hare and the tortoise, except in this instance both the hare and the tortoise can win – they just do it their way.

Are you simply born to trade?

This is a question I often get asked, especially once I've gone through some of the key aspects of the psychological make-up of the best traders and investors.

Again, the answer is both yes and no. Some are pure naturals at this game – you would say they were born to it. With others, it comes from their environment; how they were brought up. Some can learn it from books. Some pick it up later in life as they mature and pick up life's experiences. There is no simple answer.

Most importantly though, these psychological variables are all skills that can be learned. To be a success in trading and investing you do not need all of them. There are also different levels of success. There is a big difference between becoming the next Warren Buffett or making a sum from investing to pay a deposit down on your next car!

So, you should put it into perspective; you have to be realistic. What you must do is have an awareness of what it takes to succeed. As with any of life's endeavours, to get positive results you must be aware of your own strengths and weaknesses and of those whom you are competing against. By doing this you create your edge!

So can you become part of the winning set?

Yes, you can, but it is going to be hard work and require a bit of luck – luck that you create. It is not an exclusive club with a restrictive membership waiting list. Anybody can be a member.

How do you achieve trading and investing glory?

The winners in trading and investing, got to where they wanted to get, however hard their journey was. Trading and investing glory will only materialise for you, if you understand and master yourself and the playing field in which you do battle. If you don't, your results will be negative, frustrating and not meet your expectations.

It can be a cold, miserable place to be at times, but the upside can be like no other. If trading and investing was a place where winning was easy, then everyone would be doing it. In fact, if it was easy to win then eventually it would become impossible to win and the game would die.

I suggest that the best ways to enhance your chances of success in trading and investing, from a psychological viewpoint, would be to:

- Get as much experience as you can
- Become a smart thinker
- Become a trading psychopath
- Stay motivated
- Be focused and prepared
- Be resilient

I will nearly end on one final quote from a Billy Ocean song of the 1980's:

"When the going gets tough, the tough get going."

What you put in, will be what you get out and you can seriously help yourself by putting yourself in the best place(s) to succeed.

Utilising the power of the proverb!

The purpose of this book was to give you, the reader, some inspiration and motivation to get you on the right path to trading and investing success.

The wise words in this book put together in the forms of proverbs, sayings, quotes, idioms and mottos over the millennia, are very powerful tools of change. If you can embrace them and relate them to your own world, you will give yourself a better chance to succeed.

Success in this space can come down to very fine margins and anything you can do to push the odds and probabilities in your favour must be a good thing.

So, to utilise the power of the proverb, you must follow the simple three step process we outlined at the beginning of this book:

1. STOP
2. THINK
3. ACTION

As discussed in chapter 3, positive emotions and thoughts can seriously improve your cognition, attention, adaptability and smart thinking.[5,6] They encourage learning; making you more able to cope under pressure, deal with adversity, making you more proactive, giving you better coping mechanisms and in turn seriously improving your performance.

Positive emotions developed by utilising the power of the proverb can quite simply change your life and make you feel good both for the now and for the future and allow you to cope with the hidden possible dangers waiting for you in the markets. So, what appears to be a simple, insignificant proverb, saying, quote, motto or idiom can actually give you these positive, constructive emotions that are crucial to your success in the world of trading and investing.

As you navigate the ups and downs of the financial markets, or even life in general, keep this book handy. Whenever you find your positivity waning, have another flick through it. Who knows, the power of the proverb may just help.

Good luck!

GLOSSARY

Behavioural Analysis: Studies the effects of psychological, social, cognitive and emotional factors on the economic decisions of individuals and institutions and the consequences for market prices, returns, and the resource allocation.

Commodity market: A commodity market is a physical or virtual marketplace for buying, selling and trading raw or primary products e.g. gold, oil, corn etc.

Diversification: Diversification is a technique that mixes a wide variety of investments within a portfolio to control potential risk and limit losses.

Edge: The mathematical and statistical advantage you have over the 'house', in this case the market, with your trading strategies. Statistically, a 1% edge in the long run means you'll be a winner.

Fat Fingers: Verb; the act of performing a typo. In trading it means keying in, or executing the wrong trade details.

Financial Markets: A market in which people trade financial securities, commodities, and other items at prices that reflect supply and demand. Securities include stocks, bonds, and commodities.

Fundamental Analysis: A process of valuation determining the intrinsic value or real worth of an asset by examining related economic, financial and other qualitative and quantitative factors. For example, in Foreign Exchange markets analysis focuses on the overall state of the economy, and considers factors including interest rates, production, earnings, employment, GDP, housing, manufacturing and management.

Guru: A Sanskrit term. Someone who is a "teacher, guide, expert, or master" of a certain knowledge or field.

Hedge Fund: An investment fund managed by a professional investment management firm, that pools capital from accredited individuals or institutional investors across various assets and often constructed using complex portfolio and risk management techniques. Normally they are low on regulation.

Investing: To allocate money in the expectation of some benefit in the future.

Investor: A person who commits capital with the expectation of financial returns.

Losses: Trades and investments that don't make money!

Markets: See 'Financial Markets'.

Mindset: A fixed mental attitude or disposition that predetermines a person's responses to and interpretations of situations.

Money Management: In trading and investing it is the skill of maximising every winning trade, whilst minimising losses through strategic trade and risk management.

Portfolio: A collection of assets held by an institution or a private individual.

Probability: Is the measure of the likelihood that an event will occur. (Usually expressed as a percentage or ratio)

Psychology: Is the study of behaviour and mind, embracing all aspects of conscious and unconscious experience as well as thought.

Psychopath: A person with an antisocial personality disorder, especially one manifested in perverted, criminal, or amoral behaviour. In trading, we are looking for the 'good functional' psychopath and not the mass murderer!

Risk: The possibility of losing some or all of the original investment. The possibility an investment's actual return will differ from the expected return.

Risk Management: The identification, assessment and prioritisation of risks, followed by coordinated and economical application of resources, to minimize, monitor and control the probability and/or impact of unfortunate events or to maximize the realisation of opportunities. The art of keeping the shirt on your back!

Sentiment: The feeling of a particular market, or its crowd psychology, as revealed through the activity and price movement of the securities traded in that market.

Statistics: The study of the collection, analysis, interpretation, presentation and organisation of data.

Stock market: The market for trading equities or shares.

Strategy: A set of trading rules that are constructed around an idea or uncertainty that you are trying to benefit from.

Technical Analysis: The study of market action (price/volume/open interest) primarily using charts for forecasting and anticipating future price trends.

The tape: See 'Ticker tape'.

Ticker tape: Computerised device that relays to investors around the world the stock symbol and the latest price and volume on securities as they are traded.

Trading: A proactive style of buying and selling assets, both physical and financial, on domestic and international financial markets.

Trader: A person engaged in the process of trading.

Volatility: A measure of risk based on the standard deviation or variance of the asset return.

REFERENCES

1. LEFEVRE Edwin, 2010, Reminiscences of a Stock Operator, Annotated Edition, John Wiley & Sons.
2. OLIVER Stone Film, "Wall Street", 1987, TWENTIETH CENTURY FOX,
3. DUTTON Dr Kevin & MCNAB Andy, The Good Psychopaths Guide to Success, Penguin Random House UK, 2014.
4. FULLER Thomas
5. ASPINWALL, 1998, 2001: ISEN, 1990
6. TUGADE & FREDRICKSON 1998, FREDRICKSON & JOINER 2000, FREDRICKSON & BRANIGAN 2000.
7. BUENA VISTA PICTURES "The Color of Money" 1986,
8. NBC, "Star Trek", TV Series, Gene Roddenberry,
9. www.kcfortunecookiefactory.com, www.insidermonkey.com/blog/the-40-best-fortune-cookie-sayings,
10. JONES II Paul Tudor, Forbes. 2016, Retrieved 2016/10.
11. SULLIVAN, Aline, December 20, 1997, "Buffett, the Sage of Omaha, Makes Value Strategy Seem Simple: Secrets of a High Plains Investor". International Herald Tribune.
12. LEFEVRE Edwin, 1923, Reminiscences of a Stock Operator. p. 14.
13. ALLPORT, Gordon, 1935, "Attitudes," in A Handbook of Social Psychology, ed. C. Murchison. Worcester, MA: Clark University Press, 789–844.
14. JUNG, Carl G, 1971, Psychological Types. Princeton, New Jersey: Princeton University Press. ISBN 0-691-01813-8.
15. GLADWELL M, Outliers, 2008, The Story of Success, Penguin Group.

16. AMERICAN PSYCHOLOGICAL ASSOCIATION, 2014, The Road to Resilience.

17. RUTTER, M, 2008, "Developing concepts in developmental psychopathology", pp. 3–22 in J.J. Hudziak (ed.), Developmental psychopathology and wellness: Genetic and environmental influences. Washington, DC: American Psychiatric Publishing

18. SELIGMAN, M E.P.: Csikszentmihalyi, Mihaly, 2000, "Positive Psychology: An Introduction". American Psychologist.

19. KLEIN, S, 2006, The Science of Happiness. Marlowe & Company. ISBN 1-56924-328-X.

20. Image from Wikimedia Commons, record creator: department of Defence, Author Unknown, Source: US national Archives and Record Administration

21. JOURNAL OF BUSINESS AND MANAGEMENT "Risk Management - An Analytical Study" (PDF). IOSR. Feb 2014. pp. 83–89. Retrieved 6 June 2016.

22. KOCH Richard, 2007, The 80/20 Principle, The Secret of Achieving More with Less, Nicholas Brealey Publishing.

BIBLIOGRAPHY

1. LARRY PESAVANTO WITH LESLIE JOUFLAS, Essentials of Trading, Traders Press Inc, 2004.
2. DEAN LUNDELL, Sun Tzu's Art of war for traders and investors, McGraw-Hill, 1997.
3. EDWIN LEFEVRE, Reminiscences of a Stock Operator, Annotated Edition, John Wiley & Sons, 2010.
4. DR KEVIN DUTTON & ANDY MCNAB, The Good Psychopaths Guide to Success, Penguin Random House UK, 2014.
5. STEVE WARD, Trader Mind, Get a Mindful Edge in the Markets, Wiley, 2015.
6. MARK B FISHER, The Logical Trader, Applying a method to the madness Wiley Trading, 2002.
7. LARS TVEDE, The Psychology of Finance, Understanding the behavioural dynamics of markets, Wiley Trading, 2007.
8. MALCOLM GLADWELL, Outliers, The Story of Success, Penguin Group, 2008.
9. ANTHONY ROBBINS, Unlimited Power, The New Science of Personal Achievement, Simon & Schuster Inc, 2001.
10. ANTHONY ROBBINS, Awaken the Giant Within, Anthony Robbins, Simon & Schuster Inc, 2001.
11. BORIS JOHNSON, The Churchill Factor, How One Man Made History, Hodder & Stoughton, 2014.
12. MARTIN GILBERT, Churchill: The Power of Words, Bantam Press, 2012.
13. ROBERT T. KIYOSAKI, Rich Dad Poor Dad, Plata Publishing, 2011.
14. PAUL NEGRI, The Wit and Wisdom of Mark Twain, Dover Publications, 1999.
15. ROSEMARIE JARSKI, The Funniest Thing You Never Said: Ultimate Collection of Humorous Quotations, Ebury Press, 2004.

16. PEGGY ANDERSON, Great quotes from Great Leaders, The Career Press Inc, 1997.
17. CHRISTOPHER HIBBERT, Disraeli: A Personal History, Harper Perennial, 2010.
18. DAMIAN HUGHES, Five Steps to a Winning Mindset: What Sport Can Teach Us About Great Leadership, Macmillan, 2016.
19. STEPHEN LAW, The Great Philosophers: The Lives and Ideas of History's Greatest Thinkers, Quercus Publishing, 2007
20. PAUL STRATHERN, Nietzsche: Philosophy in an Hour, Harper Press, 2012.
21. GARD DE LEY, Confucius for Today: A Century of Chinese Proverbs, Robert Hale Ltd, 2009.
22. THEODORA LAU, Best Loved Chines Proverbs (2nd Edition), Collins Reference, 2009.
23. WALTER ISAACSON, Einstein: His Life and Universe, Simon & Schuster, 2008.
24. Einstein: The World as I see It, Citadel Press, 2008.
25. CHARLES CONRAD, The Way to Wealth: Ben Franklin on Money and Success, CreateSpace Independent Publishing, 2011,
26. ORMOND SEAVEY, Benjamin Franklin: Autobiography and Other Writings, OUP Oxford, 2008.
27. ROBERT SLATER, Soros: The Life, Ideas, and Impact of the World's Most Influential Investor, McGraw-Hill, 2009.
28. ALICE SCHROEDER, The Snowball: Warren Buffett and the Business of Life, Bloomsbury Publishing, 2009.
29. LAWRENCE CUNINGHAM, The Essays of Warren Buffett: Lessons for Investors and Managers, John Wiley & Sons, 2013.
30. ALEXANDER ELDER, Trading for a Living: Psychology, Trading, Tactics and Money Management, Wiley Finance, 1993.
31. DAVID MARANISS, When Pride Still Mattered: A Life of Vince Lombardi, Simon & Schuster, 2000.
32. ALISON PRICE, Psychology of Success: You're a-Z Map to Achieving Your Goals and Enjoying the Journey, Icon Books, 2016.

ABOUT THE STOP HUNTER

THE **STOP HUNTER** was founded by Stephen Hoad in January 2015, to provide professional education and training for private investors and traders.

We run courses and seminars throughout Kent, London & the South East for those who want to learn to trade the financial markets. Based on behavioural psychology, risk management and technical analysis, our courses equip you with the knowledge & skills to expertly trade the Commodities, Equities & Forex markets. Ongoing support is provided through our Traders Club.

THE **STOP HUNTER** also provides consultancy and professional services to financial institutions and universities. Our key areas of expertise are technical analysis, systematic trading, risk management and trading.

To find out more about THE **STOP HUNTER** and the services we provide take a look at our YouTube channel:

https://www.youtube.com/watch?v=El-7x5Eiuh4

Or visit our website:

https://www.thestophunter.co.uk

For all the latest market news, analysis and insights you can follow us on Twitter:

https://twitter.com/thestophunt3r

THANK YOU

Before you go I'd like to say a big thank you for purchasing my book.

If you liked what you read then I need your help – please take a moment to leave a review for this book on Amazon.

If you loved it, please tell me! You can email me at info@thestophunter.co.uk

The feedback you give will help me to continue to write books and content on trading and investing that will help you get results.

READER OFFER

Did you know that we provide weekly market analysis reports and ongoing coaching to a growing community of traders and investors, through our Traders Club?

To download a FREE copy of our weekly trade report visit https://thestophunter.co.uk/members/

You can also join our Traders Club for a FREE 1 month trial with no obligation - simply use coupon code TT30 when signing up.

If you choose to attend our Core Trader Training Programme, you can receive £200 off by quoting ref: TT200 when booking.

INDEX

(BY AUTHOR OF QUOTE)

A

AAMES William 74,
ABRAMOVIC Marina 36,
ACHARD Marcel 79,
ADAMS John Quincy 67,
ADIDAS 58,
ALCOTT Louisa May 33,
ALI Mohammed 58,86,
ANCIENT Roman Proverb 84,
ANDERSON Greg 54,
ANDRETTI Mario 52,
ANISTON Jennifer 37,
APPLE INC 76,
ARISTOTLE 22,23,140,141,
ARMANI Giorgio 47,
ARNOTT Robert 124,
ASHE Arthur 56,57,
AUGUSTINE Norman Ralph 84,
AURELIUS Marcus 93,141,
AUSTEN Jane 41,

B

BADEN-POWELL Robert 56,
BAILEY David 20,
BALDWIN Tom 124,
BANA Eric 40,

BELL Alexander Graham 69,
BENIOFF Marc 69,
BENNETT Manu 48,
BERMAN Howard 55,
BLAKE William 21,
BODHIDHARMA 35,
BOGLE Jack 124,
BONAPARTE Napoleon 58,
BOVEE Christian Nestell 34,
BRADBURY Ray 79,
BRADLEY Bill 71,
BRANDEN Nathaniel 68,
BRAULT Robert 76,
BROOKE Beth 90,
BROWN Les 86,91,
BROWN Paul 90,
BROWN Rita Mae 24,
BRYAN Sabrina 54,
BRYANT Paul 90,
BUFFETT Warren 20,119,120,
BUSCH Douglas 76,
BUSEY Gary 91,
BUTLER Nicholas M 66,

C

CAESAR Julius 24,140,
CAM Albert 23,
CANFIELD Jack 110,
CANNING George 42,
CANTONA Eric 35,
CAPOTE Truman 43,
CARMACK John 55,
CARNEGIE Dale 34,39,

CASCIO Jamais 62,
CAZIEZEL Jim 54,
CHANNING William Ellery 63,
CHENAULT Kenneth 55,
CHESTERTON Gilbert 36,
CHICAGO TRIBUNE 65,
CHILDRE Doc 61,
CHINESE PROVERB 69,135,137, 38, 139,
CHOUDHURY Bikram
CHURCHILL Sir Winston 33,50,68,90,92,94,108,109,
CIORAN Emile M 34,
CLEMENS Roger 65,
COBBETT William 67,
COFFIN William Sloane 79,
COLEMAN Langston 40,
CONANT James Bryant 80,
CONFUCIUS 57, 72,108,136,137,
COOK Dane 61,
COOK Tim 55,
COOLEY Mason 100,
COOPER Jeff 77,
COUSINS Norman 72,107,
COVEY Stephen 50,69,
CRAMER Jim 94,
CROSBY Sidney 54,
CURIE Marie 34,

D

DALI Salvador 33,
D'ANGELO Anthony J 59,
DARWIN Charles 68,
DA VINCI Leonardo 25,
DE BONO Edward 62,

DEMOCRITUS 141,
DE SALES Saint Francis 71,
DEWEY John 86,
DIAMANDIS Peter 106,
DISNEY Walt 65,
DISRAELI Benjamin 67,69,105,
DONAIRE Nonito 84,
DOREN Mark Van 58,
DORGAN Bryan 76,
DUHIGG Charles 79,
D'URFEY Thomas 37,
DRUCKER Peter 52,
DUTCH PROVERB 71,
DYER Wayne 62,

E

EDISON Thomas 27,42,70,92,
EDWARDS Elizabeth 63,
EINSTEIN Albert 20,23,58,59,95,99,103,107,
EISENHOWER Dwight D 110,
ELDER (Dr) Alexander 26,103,125,
ELLIOTT Nicole 108,
ELLIOTT Walter 67,
ELLIS Albert 75,
EMERSON Ralph Waldo 24,34,40,56,59,67,70,109,
EPICTETUS 94,141,
EVERTON FOOTBALL CLUB 52,

F

FEATHER William 53,
FIORINA Carly 79,
FORBES BC 87,

FORBES Malcolm S 66,
FRANCE Anatole 85,
FRANKLIN Benjamin 20,39,40,42,56,59,
FREIDMAN Milton 87,
FREIRE Paulo 22,
FREUD Sigmund 36,
FROST Robert 27,
FROSTRUP Mariella 75,
FULLER Thomas 40,86,

G

GABELLI Mario 106,
GABLE Dan 89,
GALEANO Eduardo 107,
GANN William D 103,123,
GARLAND Judy 25,
GARDNER John W 23, 107,
GATES Bill 42,76,
GIAEVER Ivar 75,
GIDE Andre 78,
GINGRICH Newt 67,
GLADWELL Malcolm 23,
GODIN Seth 77,
GOLDEN Harry 40,
GOLEMAN Daniel 54,
GEKKO Gordon (from the film Wall Street) 32,101,103,
GRAHAM Benjamin 125,
GRANDIN Temple 68,
GRAY Gary E. 48,
GRETZKY Wayne 80,
GRIFFIN III Robert 64,
GRYLLS Bear 61,
GIULIANI Rudy 95,

H

HADFIELD Chris 79,
HALL Tom T 91,
HARDY Thomas 34,
HARE Robert D 81,
HARRISON George 37,
HARRIS Sydney J 22,
HARRIS Thomas 35,
HAWKING Stephen 63,
HAUERWAS Stanley 35,
HAYES Woody 66,
HERACLITUS 26,68,140,141,
HERBERT George 80,
HERODOTUS 41,
HERTZ Noreena 54,
HILL Napoleon 33,51
HITE Larry 105,123,
HOAD Stephen 37,101 - 107,109,
HOLTZ Lou 91,
HONDA 83,
HUCKABEE Mike 61,
HUBBARD Elbert 38,75,
HUGO Victor 93,

I

INGERSOLL Robert Green 44,
IRISH ARMY CAVALRY CORPS 49,
ISAACSON Walter 77,

J

JAMAICAN PROVERB 79,
JAPANESE PROVERB 66,79,86,102,129 - 131,
JAMES William 80 - 82,
JAMESON Jenna 34,
JEFFERSON Thomas 22,52,
JOBS Steve 54,
JOHNSON John H 77,
JOHNSON Lyndon B 65,
JOHNSON Samuel 66,
JOHNSON Shawn 55,
JONES Paul Tudor 117 - 118,
JORDAN Michael 42,54,65,70,
JOYCE James 39,
JUNG Karl 85,

K

KAHNEMAN Daniel 65,
KANE Patrick 26,
KEATS John 25,
KEMPTON Sally 48,
KENNEDY John F 40,
KEYNES John Maynard 101,102,
KHAN Jahangir 53,
KIERKEGAARD Soren 23,
KING Billy Jean 89,
KING Stephen 22,
KIRN Walter 38,
KITT Eartha 35,
KIYOSAKI Robert 47,71,
KLINE Richard 70,
KORDA Michael 86,

KOVNER Bruce 108,125,

L

LAKEIN Alan 110 - 111,
LAMA Dalai 57,65,
LANDRY Tom 73,
LAUGHIN Owen 78,
LEE Bruce 39,
LEONARD Sugar Ray
LEONARD Thomas 55,74,
LEVENSTEIN Aaron 109,
LEWIS CARL 89,
LIN Maya 63,
LINCOLN Abraham 80,
LIPSCHUTZ Bill 123,
LIVELY Blake 70,
LIVERMORE Jesse 19,101,103 - 104,120 - 121,
LO Andrew 106,
LOMBARDI Vince 23,52,70,88 - 90,
LOU, WALL STREET 41,105,
LOVECRAFT H.P. 33,
LYNCH Peter 123,
LYND Robert Staughton 20,

M

MACARTHUR Douglas 40,
MACGILL Patrick 40,
MADDEN Steve 35,
MAIMONIDES 141,
MALCOLM X 93,
MALTZ Maxwell 39,
MAMIS Justin 123,

MANDELA Nelson 22,87,
MARQUIS Don 78,
MARTENSSON Jonatan 61,
MAXWELL John C 53,77,
MCCOY Tony 91,
MCDOWELL Josh 55
MCENROE John 89,
MCMAHON Tim 79,
MELLON Tamara 34,51,
MICHELANGELO 58,
MILANO Alyssa 90,
MILLIGAN Spike 87,
MILNE AA 22,
MIZNER Wilson 38,
MOLIERE 71,
MONTGOMERY L.M. 93,
MOORE Mary Tyler 39,
MORISSETTE Alanis 36,
MOSES Edwin 89,
MU Du 61,
MURDOCK Mike 42,
MURRAY Andy 54,

N

NAISBITT John 108,
NAMATH Joe 70,
NASSAR David 47,
NAVRATILOVA Martina 52,
NEILL Humphrey B 122,
NELSON Willie 109,
NEHRU Jawaharlal 72,78,
NELSON Byron 73,
NEO-CLASSICAL BEHAVIOURAL FINANCE 101,

NICHOLSON William 25,
NIETSCHE Freidrich 36,63,66,94,
NIKE INC. 53,
NIN Anais 26,
NIXON Richard M 74,
NORMAN Donald 57,
NORTH Edmund H 79,
NORTON Edward 79,

O

OBAMA Barack 93,
OCEAN Billy 148,
O'NEILL William 123,125,
ORTBERG John 67
ORWELL George 108,
OSBORNE George 63,
O'SHAUGHNESSY James 31,
OSLER William 24,
OWENS Jesse 85,89,

P

PALMER Arnold 70,90,92,
PARSONS Bob 65,
PATTON George S 53,92,102,
PAUL II Pope John 93,
PAULSON John 124,
PELE 67,
PETER Lawrence J 86,
PERON Evita 108,
PHELPS Michael 89,
PICASSO Pablo 82,
PICKENS T.Boone 37,124,

PITINO Rick 42,
PORTER Michael 110,
POWELL Colin 36,56,66,92,
POWELL John 38,

Q

QUBEIN Nido 68,

R

RAND Ayn 87,
RASCHKE Linda Bradford 86,122,
REAGAN Ronald 34,
RIDE Sally 24,
RILEY Pat 51,
ROBBINS Anthony (Tony) 43,52,55,59,73,85 - 86,92,
ROCKEFELLER Jr John D 92,
RODGERS Bill 74,
ROLLINS Henry 49,
ROHN Jim 21,51,53,61,86,
ROONEY Mickey 92,
ROOSEVELT Theodore 58,
ROSSI Valentino 110,
ROTH Philip 101,
ROYAL AIR FORCE 52,
ROZMAN Deborah 61,
RUSH Ian 33,
RUSKIN John 24,
RUTH Babe 89,
RYUN Jim 84,

S

SAADI OF SHIRAZ 71,
SAMUELSON Paul 125,
SANDBURG Carl 85,
SANTAYANA 107,
SANTOS DE LIMA Lucimar 66,
SCHULLER Robert H 56,67,
SCHUMACHER Ernst F 23,
SCHUMACHER Michael 84,
SCHWAGER Jack D 122,
SCHWARTZ David Joseph 33,
SCHWARTZ Marty 106,122,
SCOTT Walter 50,
SENECA Lucius Annaeus 34,40,57,140,
SEUSS Dr 62,
SEYKOTA Ed 124,
SHAKESPEARE William 21,82,
SHAW George Bernard 101,
SHAY R.E. 37,
SHEDD William G.T. 80,
SHEEHY Gail 68,
SHER Barbara 80,
SHORT Solomon 77,
SIMPSON Alan K 63,
SINETAR Marsh 87,
SINGLETARY Mike 89,
SLASH 79,
SPENCER Herbert 22,
SPITZ Mark 73,
SNEAD Samuel 23,
SOCRATES 25,141,
SOLO Hope 70,
SOROS George 115,118,

SPECIAL AIR SERVICE (SAS) 49,
SPRINGSTEEN Bruce 41,
STANTON Elizabeth Cady 75,
STAR TREK (TV SHOW) 83,
STENGEL Casey 89,
STEPANEK Mattie 93,
STERNLICHT Barry 74,
STEVENSON Adlai E 87,
STONE W. Clement 62,
STOWE Beecher 66,
STRAUSS Neil 51,
STREISAND Barbara 25,
SURTEES John 73,
SWEDISH PROVERB 39,
SWEENEY Paul 33,
SWIFT Jonathan 35,
SYRUS Pubilius 38,52,140 - 141,

T

TEMPLETON Sir John 124,
THATCHER Margaret 88,
THE COLOUR OF MONEY 38,
THOMAS Isaiah 73,
THOMPSON Hunter S 38,77,
TOBEL Alexa Von 111,
TOLLE Eckhart 55,
TOLSTOY Leo 71,
TOTTENHAM HOTSPUR 49,
TRACEY Brian 65,90,
TRUMAN Harry 31,
TRUMP Donald 41,87,
TURNER Sophie 94,
TUSSER Thomas 88,

173

TWAIN Mark 21 - 22,24,44,87,101 - 102,104,107,
TZU Lau 15,21,76,82,90,110,135,
TZU Sun 19,110,131,133 - 134,

U

UNITED STATES ARMY 49,
UNKNOWN 80,84,102,106,107,
UNSER Robert 56,

V

VOLTAIRE 24,93,
VON GOETHE Johann Wolfgang 67,

W

WAGNER Richard 58,
WAITLEY Denis 69,91,
WALSCH Neale Donald 69,
WAMBACH Abby 84,
WANG An 74,
WARD William Arthur 89,
WATKINS James N 66,
WEBB Marie 85,
WEIL Andrew 31,
WELCH Jack 68,94,
WEST Jessamyn 107,
WILDE Oscar 25,27,
WILLIAMS Bernard 63,
WILLIAMS Evan 77,
WILLIAMS Roy H 76,
WILSON Earl 40,

WILSON Woodrow 102,
WOODEN John 24,65,69,76,90,
WOOTTEN Morgan 90,
WOLF Naomi 63,
WORDSWORTH William 94,
WRIGHT Frank Lloyd 57,

Y

YOGANANDA Paramahansa 42,

Printed in Great Britain
by Amazon